# Getting Started in
# Mass Media

Christine Beckert
Ashland High School
Ashland, Massachusetts

National Textbook Company
a division of *NTC Publishing Group* • Lincolnwood; Illinois USA

**Cover Photo Credits**

*Top left:* Photo courtesy of Foote, Cone & Belding Communications, Inc.
*Middle left:* Photo courtesy of Hughes Communications, Inc.
*Bottom left:* Photographer, Bob Glaze/ARTSTREET, Chicago
*Right:* Artist's rendering courtesy of National Aeronautics and Space Administration

# Acknowledgments

"The Fun They Had" by Isaac Asimov. Reprinted by permission of the author. "Tooth and Man" by Russell Baker. Copyright © 1982 by The New York Times Company. Reprinted by permission.

"Radio, the Parent Reborn" by Les Brown from ELECTRIC MEDIA by Les Brown and Dr. Sema Marks, copyright © 1974 by Harcourt Brace Jovanovich, Inc., reprinted by permission of the publisher.

"The Rise of the Couch Potato" from MAKING SENSE by Ellen Goodman. Copyright © 1989 by the Washington Post Company. Used by permission of Atlantic Monthly Press.

"Shoe" cartoon by Jeff MacNelly reprinted by permission: Tribune Media Services.

"Now you just slide in the disc and watch the plot thicken" by Bruce McCabe. Reprinted courtesy of the *Boston Globe*.

"Go to the head of the class" from LIFE, AND OTHER WAYS TO KILL TIME . . . by Mike Nichols. Published by arrangement with Carol Publishing Group. A Lyle Stuart Book.

"Where There's Smoke" from NOT THAT YOU ASKED by Andrew A. Rooney. Copyright © 1989 by Essay Productions, Inc. Reprinted by permission of Random House, Inc.

"Editors Who Leave Too Much" by John Playsted Wood, senior editor, *Modern Maturity* magazine. This essay appeared in *Writer's Digest* magazine (January 1991) and is from THE GREAT GLUT: PUBLIC COMMUNICATION IN THE UNITED STATES by John Playsted Wood, published by Thomas Nelson Publishers. Reprinted by permission.

**1996 Printing**

Published by National Textbook Company, a division of NTC Publishing Group.
©1992 by NTC Publishing Group, 4255 West Touhy Avenue,
Lincolnwood (Chicago), Illinois 60646-1975 U.S.A.
Library of Congress Catalog Card Number: 91–61816
Manufactured in the United States of America.

6 7 8 9 0 VP 9 8 7 6 5 4

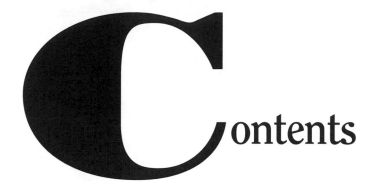

# Contents

# Preface

The mass media are among the most pervasive features of modern life. They inform, amuse, startle, anger, thrill,—but very seldom leave anyone untouched.

*Getting Started in Mass Media* helps you understand these influences, both the media themselves and their messages. Organized around individual media, each chapter provides the base needed to become intelligent consumers of media. Multiple activities call on you to think, write, explore, and evaluate. Keeping a notebook as you work through the media activities in this book is recommended. In each chapter a section called "Talking It Over" provides a forum for debate on some of the key issues in media today. Each chapter also includes a "Viewpoint" section, which contains a reading. The readings are selections from other authors who provide perspective, often with a humorous touch. Although the author and publisher of *Getting Started in Mass Media* do not necessarily agree with the opinions expressed, these selections give you further food for thought and encourage you to use humor to make a point.

In the years to come, media will become more pervasive—not less—and understanding of their operation and influence will be crucial to wise use. *Getting Started in Mass Media* seeks to spark that knowledge and understanding.

# Introduction to Mass Media

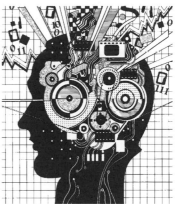

> **W**e have, as it were, to live in a global village.
>
> —Marshall McLuhan

## Mass Media

Perhaps you woke up this morning with your radio alarm set to your favorite station. Maybe you played a tape while you showered and dressed. While you ate breakfast, you may have skimmed the front page of the morning newspaper. On the bus on the way to school, you may have seen a poster advertising a new toothpaste. During social studies class you went to the library and checked out books and consulted magazines you needed for a research project. In science class you watched a film about arctic wolves. When you arrived home, you flopped on the couch and watched television for a while. The ads annoyed you, but you were interested enough in the show to put up with them.

Each of these experiences put you in contact with a **medium,** or channel, of communication. Radio, records and tapes, newspapers, billboards, books, magazines, movies, television, advertising—all of these are **mass media** because they reach many people at one time.

Mass media have an enormous impact. They have become so important, in fact, that they are often called simply "the media," as if other, personal media had shrunk in importance.

### Activity 1

Reserve one section of your notebook for a **media log,** in which you will record your own media experiences as you proceed through this course. As your first entry, create a chart of the following media: television, movies (including videotapes), radio, audio recordings (records, tapes, CD's), newspapers, magazines, and books. Now estimate how many hours per week you spend with each medium. Be prepared to explain how you arrived at your estimates as you discuss them with your classmates. With which medium do you personally spend the most time? Why? Which media are most significant to the class as a whole?

# Communication Process

Say your friend is absentmindedly about to step into a busy intersection. "Watch out!" you scream. He stops, and you may have prevented an accident— simple, right? But think about what happened.

First, you had an image in your mind of your friend's danger. In a moment you had to choose a method of warning him. Your medium of communication might have been a shove, a note, or a wave of your arms. You decided to shout, but then you had to decide what words to use. Assuming you screamed "Watch out!" loudly enough for your friend to hear, it then becomes his job to interpret your message. If he does not speak English, your words may mean nothing to him. If he is caught up in his own thoughts, he may ignore you. If he is thinking about his girlfriend on the other side of the intersection, he may misinterpret your warning. If he correctly interprets your words, however, his mind will instantly focus and he will stop—with luck, before he has an accident, or causes one.

A lot has gone on in just a few seconds. Is it any wonder, then, that problems arise when people try to communicate more complicated messages? The true marvel is that people often do communicate remarkably well despite these difficulties.

Let's look at a diagram of the communication process.

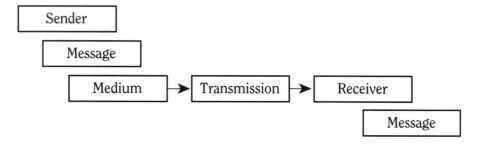

In any communication, the sender decides on the message and chooses a medium—a channel—of communication. The sender transmits—sends—the message to a receiver, who must recreate the message in his or her own mind. The message in the receiver's mind, however, may be different from the message the sender intended. Communication has occurred regardless of the message in the receiver's mind, but from the sender's point of view, the communication is successful only if the message received closely resembles the message sent.

Problems can occur at any step in the communication process. The sender may frame the message confusingly or may choose an inappropriate medium. Writing a letter of complaint to a local grocery store, for example, may not be as effective as visiting the manager in person. **Interference**—like a PA announcement during your speech to your English class—may get in the way of effective transmission. The receiver may be receiving too many messages at once—a problem called **overload.** If you are talking to your friend Consuela while she has the radio on and while her mother is also trying to talk to her, for example, your message may get lost in the overload. A final problem may be the receiver's inability to understand or interpret the message.

Essentially, mass media messages are communicated by the same process as individual messages, with one important difference. When you tell your friend crossing the street to "Watch out!" he can respond by stopping or by replying, "Thanks." You receive instant **feedback.** But the mass media, so far at least, transmit only one-way communications. The feedback you might give to the sender—in the form of a letter or the purchase of a product—is delayed. Unlike personal communication, there is no immediate give-and-take between sender and receiver. Forecasters of tomorrow, however, say that the day of two-way mass communication is not far off.

**Activity 2**

Brainstorm for specific examples of problems in personal communication that can arise during each of the following steps in the process:

- as the sender frames a message
- as the sender chooses a medium
- as the message is being transmitted
- as the message is being received
- as the receiver interprets the message

# Purposes of Communication

Most messages can be classified by purpose: to inform, to persuade, or to entertain. And many messages serve more than one purpose. When you write a letter to your cousin in Florida, for example, you may want to inform her of your doings and persuade her to visit you this summer, while you entertain her with your writing style.

Messages from the mass media are also intended to inform, persuade, and entertain. Radio announcements might inform listeners about community events. Your textbooks seek to inform you about language, science, and history.

Other messages are supposed to persuade, to change people's minds or to move them to act. A television ad may urge viewers to eat a certain kind of hamburger. A magazine article may encourage teenagers to stay in school.

Still other communications are designed to entertain. A comic book lets readers escape into a fantasy land. A movie lets viewers experience life from another point of view for a while.

Mass media messages, too, can serve more than one purpose. That magazine article about staying in school must also include enough information to prove its point. A radio ad may be even more persuasive if it is also entertaining.

And many messages communicated by the mass media must serve a fourth purpose: to make money. Communications is a noble profession, but as a wise consumer you must remember that it is a business, too. A publishing house that loses money every year will not publish books for long. On the other hand, books and movies that net their producers fortunes may well generate sequels. Profits affect what you receive from the media.

**Activity 3**

1. Find and clip a newspaper article whose primary purpose is to inform, one whose primary purpose is to persuade, and one whose primary purpose is to entertain. Be prepared to defend your choices.

2. Find and bring to class an example of a magazine article that you believe has at least two purposes.

3. Prepare to discuss these questions. (You may find the log you prepared for Activity 1 helpful.)

   a. From which mass media do you gain most of your information?

   b. Which mass media do you usually turn to for entertainment? Why?

   c. What was the last book or magazine you read for entertainment? Why was it entertaining? Was it also informative or persuasive?

   d. Can you identify an occasion when you were persuaded by a mass media message?

## Media and Culture

Communication is closely tied to culture. Once people developed language, they could discuss and agree on ways of living together in towns and cities. They could specialize in professions and pass on what they knew to young people. They could entertain each other with stories, songs, and plays.

With written language, they could learn about far away people, even if they never met them. They could found empires and pass unifying laws and promote trade. They could keep a record of events and save information for later generations.

New technologies have made mass media even more dramatic. From your living room, you can watch the results of an earthquake in China. You can see the moons of Jupiter. You can sit on your couch and read a book written three hundred years ago on the other side of the world. You can tap into a computer for a list of recent articles about artichokes.

Mass media are important in supporting democracy and in stimulating the economy. Wherever there is freedom, there is a free press that keeps people informed. And the media, which through advertising, promotes buying and selling, also supports a healthy economy.

The media have their critics, too, of course. Some say they promote shallow values, that they often misinform people, that they encourage people to consume so much that the environment is threatened.

And some social observers worry that people are being bombarded by too much information. Radio, television, books, magazines, movies, advertising—all of these are throwing words and images at you and demanding your attention. The average person may read ten thousand words each day and hear another twenty thousand on radio and television.

How do you make sense of all this information? Doing so is not an easy task. And as you grow older, there will be even more information, coming at you faster and from more sources. This is the Information Age, and you must be prepared for it.

# Talking It Over

**Make a preliminary judgment of the media. First, list as many positive and negative aspects of media as you can think of. Then decide which of the statements below better reflects your judgment. Discuss your lists and your conclusion with your classmates.**

■ On balance, the information and entertainment value of the media outweighs their negative aspects.

■ On balance, the negative effects of media on individuals and society outweigh their benefits.

# Activity 4

You already know a lot about the mass media. Television, radio, newspapers, books, magazines, and motion pictures are a part of your daily life. So the question comes up: What do you expect to learn from a course in mass media? Make a list of the information and insights you hope to gain from this course; feel free to change your list as you discuss it with your classmates and teacher. Save your list and, when you have finished the course, compare your list with what you actually learned.

## Summary

The mass media—communication channels that reach many people at once—essentially operate by the same process as personal communication: The sender frames a message, chooses a medium, and transmits the message; the receiver receives and interprets the message. Like personal communication, mass media messages may be intended to inform, to persuade, or to entertain. The media have an enormous impact on culture, past, present, and future; but they are also businesses, which must make money to survive. Wise consumers must understand not only the messages of the media, but the media themselves.

**James Playsted Wood** was a teacher, a writer for various newspapers and magazines, an advertising copywriter, and a speechwriter. His published books include adult and juvenile novels, biographies, histories, and commentary on media. In the following excerpt Wood describes the ways readers, listeners, and viewers respond to the enormous quantity of media messages that bombard them.

# The Great Glut
### James Playsted Wood

Competition [among the media] also provides the great glut, the spate that threatens to engulf and drown all of us who are communicated at. No one has a thumb large enough to plug the hole in the dike, but the individual, bombarded hourly with emotion-charged words and with television in continuous showing, does have a choice of several attitudes and actions he can adopt toward public communication.

He can wallow in it. He can luxuriate in the propaganda, the public relations handouts, the press inadequacies, the radio babble, the advertising clamor, and the smirking television prattle.

He can also ignore it. He can stop reading newspapers and magazines and turn off his radio and television. He can cover his ears against the din and go his own way and probably be no worse off. He may even do something like that, anyway, without conscious intent, which is just how mass inertia is created.

Publishers, producers, and exhibitors have worried for some time about what they call the lessening "span of attention." People cannot keep their minds on anything very long. Many of them cannot read a whole book, read or listen to a complete advertisement, or finish a magazine article. That does not mean a diminution of mental or moral powers, but is an indication of surfeit. People cannot keep their minds on things because there are too many things to keep them on. Inattention is not a vice but a protective virtue.

The individual can do something else. He can still decide what he wants to read or see and hear, and when. He can pick and choose among and within the media. In addition, he can realize certain obvious facts that we too often overlook. Public communication is consciously planned, manufactured, and sold, just like any other article of commerce. When offered for purchase, it should be viewed with the same suspicion with which you inspect anything else that is offered for sale. Look at it carefully and you will see the sound craftsmanship or the mistakes and attempts at repair.

Who said it? Why did he say it? What is he trying to do to you? No one can speak, write, or perform anything without betraying his prejudices, temperament, and intent. You have to translate all public communication in these terms. You must also know who you are and how you read or hear or see. Only at this point does communication take place.

The individual must bring all the critical intelligence of which he is capable to his acceptance or rejection of public communication. If he does, some of the amorphous mass of information may become truly intelligible and useful.

He may even come to some unexpected realizations. One is that perhaps there is nothing basically wrong with public communications at all, that what really needs changing is essential human nature, although attempts over the past few thousand years to change that have not been markedly successful.

The critical individual may also come to have an inkling of what is meant by the phrase, "In the beginning was the Word, and the Word was with God, and the Word was God." Creation began with the word. The world lives with it and by it. When the word goes, civilization will go with it. ■

## ☛ Your Turn

1. Write three short sketches, one of a person who wallows in media, one who ignores them, and one who is a discriminating consumer.

2. Your teacher will divide the class into groups of five or six. Each group should prepare a creative demonstration of the glut of media. Perhaps you could present a short play with one student as the consumer and the rest as purveyors of various media. Or, you could present a rap song that highlights the media around you.

# 2 Advertising

## The Role of Advertising

You can tell the ideals of a nation by its advertisements.

—Norman Douglas

Advertising itself is a medium—it communicates messages to consumers. But it also fuels other media. Advertising accounts for well over half of newspaper and magazine income and all of radio and non-cable television income. There are serious criticisms of advertising, as you will see, but those who want to ban it altogether must realize that newspaper and magazine prices would more than double, and all radio and television would become pay-per-use.

Advertising also helps fuel the economy. In earlier times, when products were made and consumed locally, advertising was not necessary. A signboard hung above a shop door was enough. But with the growth of mass production techniques and the spread of rail transportation in the nineteenth century, products could be sent to consumers great distances away and advertising helped to sell those products.

True, advertising adds to the cost of products, but without the mass production and mass distribution that advertising supports, the products might be even more expensive—or not available at all.

Advertising is big business in itself, a $130 billion a year industry. Because space in print and time on broadcasts are so expensive, especially in the major media (a 30-second spot on the Super Bowl can cost $700,000), advertisers choose carefully. Market researchers prepare detailed profiles of viewers, listeners, and readers—noting such characteristics as their gender, age, race, interests, and spending power. They use sophisticated techniques, including in-depth psychological studies, to find out exactly what kinds of ads will appeal to various groups. With this information, advertisers can target their purchases of media time or space to a particular audience and can design ad campaigns to appeal to that audience.

Take the youth market, for example. In 1989, children six to twelve years old spent $6 billion, and teens twelve to nineteen spent $56 billion—and not all of this money went for junk food, clothes, and records. One study showed that 60 percent of girls and 40 percent of boys do some of the family grocery shopping. In response to this finding, food marketers dramatically increased their advertising in youth magazines. Other advertisers are also trying to tap the huge youth market, spending $500 million a year on ads aimed at kids.

Adults are inundated with advertising as well. Studies show that each American is exposed to about *1,600 ad messages a day*—on television and radio, in newspapers and magazines, on billboards and signs. The sheer volume of this exposure is enough to affect people's attitudes, habits, styles, and even values.

*Activity* **1**

1. What portion of the media is advertising? Find out for yourself. Your teacher may divide the class into groups for this project.

   a. In a local newspaper, count the pages of news and entertainment. On some pages you will have to estimate—one-fourth, one-half, or three-quarters. Then count the pages of advertising. Work out the percentages of news and advertising.

   b. Do the same for a number of magazines of different types.

   c. Watch an hour of television on one of the major channels. Carefully record the number of minutes of programming and the number of minutes of advertising. Work out the percentages of programming and advertising.

   d. Do the same for several different types of radio stations, AM and FM.

   e. Compare your results with those of other groups in the class. Work out the averages, and record the results in your media log.

2. Be a media buyer. If you were the head of a life insurance company, would you advertise in *Reader's Digest* or in *Sports Illustrated?* If you wanted to sell children's vitamins, would you advertise on a radio talk show or on a Top 40s station? How about cat food—what television show would you sponsor? If you opened a pizza restaurant, where would you advertise? In each case, be prepared to explain your choice.

## The Appeal of Ads

The message of an ad is a combination of a claim and an image. The **claim** is what the advertiser says about the product. One type of claim may be

**informational,** providing specific facts about the product—what it's made of, how it works, how much it costs. Store ads and ads in catalogs are frequently of this type.

Another type of claim may attempt **product differentiation** to show how this product is different from similar products—why you should buy this toothpaste, perfume, gasoline, or cereal rather than another brand.

The **image** is the visual part of the ad, or more broadly, the feeling that the advertiser wants the viewer or reader to associate with the product.

You must be very careful as you judge a product claim. "Shine Toothpaste helps prevent cavities," an advertiser might state. But notice that the ad does not say the toothpaste *prevents* cavities, just that it *helps* prevent them—so does cleaning your teeth with baking soda. "The new T-11 car will give you a smoother ride," another says—but smoother than what? Unfinished comparisons are perfectly legal, but when you think about them, they don't say much.

Many claims are essentially meaningless. "There's no other soft drink like it" could be true, but it's probably also true of the competition. "Lip Light makes your lips glow with color" is a claim any lipstick might make. "Julep Mints taste like a whiff of springtime" leaves us asking, "What does spring taste like anyway?" "The shampoo with a touch of orange blossoms" fails to tell us what orange blossoms have to do with clean hair.

Some claims ask a rhetorical question—one that doesn't require an answer. "Wouldn't you rather have Dairy Choice ice cream?" "Shouldn't you be wearing a Time-On watch?" The advertiser wants you to think the only possible response is "Sure!" and once you believe this you will have to buy the product.

Some claims try to flatter you: "You've made it at last—now treat yourself to gold" or "Regency men's clothes—because you deserve the best." By appealing to your vanity, the advertiser wants you to associate the product with feeling good about yourself.

Some claims are rooted in so-called scientific evidence or special ingredients, but unless you know all the facts, it is wise not to take such claims too seriously. "Nine out of ten doctors surveyed recommend End-Itch for those annoying mosquito bites" offers no proof that rigorous polling methods were used. A hundred doctors could have been surveyed, but the advertiser may have chosen to highlight only ten of their responses. In truth nine out of the ten doctors *the advertiser selected* said what the advertiser wanted them to say. "The only cough drop with Nocale" may sound impressive, but Nocale may simply be a registered trade mark for an ingredient in most cough drops, or it may be an unimportant taste enhancer.

Be leery even when you "see" the evidence. You watched one car go farther with Trymore gasoline? Perhaps—but you didn't see the other driver riding his clutch to decrease his fuel efficiency.

Images the advertiser wants you to associate with the product are even harder to judge. Picture a lonely boy hanging around on the fringes of a group, or even being insulted by the other kids. He uses Sweet Breath mouthwash and suddenly the boys are clapping him on the back and the girls are falling all over him. The ad appeals to viewers' insecurities and their desire to belong; the advertiser hopes its audience credits Sweet Breath with the boy's success. You know that popularity depends on more than a clean mouth, but the image may stick, and you'll be led to buy Sweet Breath the next time you're in a drugstore.

Or picture a romantic moonlit night by the shore, a handsome young man and woman obviously in love, and a soft voice assuring you, "Love Mist perfume makes it happen." Clearly the advertiser wants you to think you'll end up on a moonlit shore if you use Love Mist. Common sense tells you many other things are necessary to get you to that shore, but the strong appeal of the image may override such logic.

The Love Mist ad is based on romantic love, but some ads are more blatant in their use of sex appeal. Many people are disturbed by the growing use of this tactic. Perfumes, clothes, deodorants, mouthwashes, even food and household cleansers are presented in sexy images to make the product seem more appealing. Wise consumers have learned to see through such images to discover what the product will really accomplish.

*A*ctivity **2**

1. Choose five print ads and five television ads (take careful notes on the television ads), and be prepared to discuss the message—the claim and the image—of each. Does it appeal to your reason, your emotions, or both?

2. Find several examples of product differentiation ads for competing brands—a number of shampoo ads, for example. According to each ad, why should you buy this brand rather than the competition?

3. Evaluate the ads you examined in exercises 1 and 2. Which make legitimate claims and present honest images of the product? Which make questionable or empty claims? Be prepared to discuss your judgment.

# Propaganda Techniques

Advertisers use a number of propaganda techniques in their claims and images. The word **propaganda** broadly covers all attempts at persuasion that are not based firmly on reason and critical thinking. Opinion molders use these techniques for good purposes and for bad. To be a smart consumer, you must be able to spot the propaganda techniques being used and judge the validity of their appeals.

**Bandwagon.** In old-time parades the circus band would ride on a wagon and attract a lot of followers; many people would try to jump on the bandwagon. Now, when an advertiser claims that "People are flocking to Blue Heaven jeans," he or she is using the bandwagon appeal to convince you to join everyone else. (So are you, when you try to persuade your parents that everyone has one or everyone is doing it.)

**Testimonial.** A testimonial is a recommendation by a celebrity or an authority. Some ads use an anonymous "expert"—an actor dressed as a doctor or a teacher or a homemaker who speaks glowingly about the aspirin or computer game or detergent. And some ads feature a big star—such as a famous athlete, actor, or singer—who recommends the product or sings its praises. Such ads are very effective—but also highly controversial. Think about it: If a star is paid $5 million to speak highly of a product as Michael Jackson was for his appearance in two ninety-second Pepsi ads, that star's recommendation may be a bit suspect.

**Plain Folks.** In a way, a plain folks appeal is the flip side of a testimonial. With this technique, the ad claims that people just like you—ordinary, everyday American teenagers, or average women or men, or typical families—can have a fine outing at Steer One Hamburger, go on a great camping trip in a Tycho van, or shine athletically in Rebound sneakers. In other words, they promise, plain folks can be special folks through the purchase of the product.

**Glittering Generality.** Here the ad associates "virtue words" or "virtue images" with the product—the product "glitters" with virtue although no direct connection between the product and the virtue is claimed. Health is a virtue to most people, so a makeup company may emphasize healthy skin and feature models glowing with health. Wealth is a virtue many people desire, so car advertisers picture their automobiles conveying elegant people to exotic mansions.

**Name Calling.** Name calling is the opposite of glittering generality. While the ad might say glowing things about one product, it associates the competitor's products with negative qualities. In politics, name calling can become vicious. In advertising, it's often used with supposed medical tests or surveys, which, as discussed before, can be misleading.

**Heartstrings.** You have probably noticed that many ads appeal to emotions—to people's need to be loved and accepted and to feel good about themselves. Some ads take this a step further by appealing directly to the heartstrings. Poignancy—feeling happy and sad at the same time—ranks high in ads today, and for good reason. A coffee ad showing two women talking about a difficult moment in their lives, a telephone ad showing a family healing its wounds—these are powerful messages indeed. You might ask yourself, however, if that special moment would have been any different if the women were drinking tea or the family were using a different telephone company.

**Activity 3**

Find an example of each propaganda technique in advertising: bandwagon, testimonial, plain folks, glittering generality, name calling, and heartstrings. Try to include some print ads and some radio or TV commercials. For the latter, try to quote the claim and take careful notes on the image.

## Other Techniques of Advertising

Advertisers will try anything to get you to spend your money. **Humor** is a mainstay in modern ads; the idea is that if you're amused by the ad, you'll pay attention rather than flip the page or switch the channel. Relatively new is the use of **mini-dramas,** a complete short story in thirty or sixty seconds. Sometimes these stories, which are usually humorous or poignant, are presented as serials—part 1 this week, part 2 the next.

**Repetition** and **slogans** are also mainstays. Consumers often claim they are annoyed by seeing the same ad over and over again. Yet when they buy, they forget the annoyance and choose a product because its name has been drilled into their heads. In the same way a slogan associated with a product—"Put a tiger in your tank," "Progress is our most important product"—can be a powerful tool when it is used over and over in different ads. A slogan is often the keynote of a whole **advertising campaign**—a series of ads with a similar message and based on similar techniques.

For radio and, especially, television ads, **music** has become increasingly important. The message might be accompanied by a simple jingle, a very good song written just for the ad, a popular song adapted to fit a product, or a full orchestra playing classical music.

Advances in **video technology** offer new techniques for advertisers, too. Computer-generated art and music, fast cuts, animation, and trick photography can dramatize the product and increase its appeal.

The quality and creativity of many ads is impressive—some people say that on TV, at least, the ads are superior to the programs. Annual awards, called **Clio awards** (Clio was the Greek Muse of history, but the name derives from a word meaning "fame, glory"), are given for outstanding radio and television commercials and print advertisements. Remember, however, that the purpose of all advertising is to snag and keep consumers' attention so that the sales message can come across. Many award-winning ads have not been good selling tools because people remember the ads but not the product!

Enjoy the high-quality ads you see and hear, but never stop being a media expert. Judge each ad for the validity of its claim; apply a critical eye to the image that's being sold; separate technique from truth. Doing so, you'll have more fun with the ads themselves. You'll have the satisfaction of psyching out those sophisticated ad people. And you'll make wiser decisions when you shop.

**Activity 4**

1. As a class, brainstorm to create a list of current slogans and jingles. Which do you think are the most effective? Can you remember the product associated with each?

2. Award class Clios to deserving TV commercials. In small groups nominate ads in the following categories: Funniest, Best Use of Music, Best Use of Video, Most Touching, Most Outrageous Overall, and Most Creative Overall. If possible, tape the ads, view and discuss their merits in class, and then vote to choose the winners.

# Ad Production

Madison Avenue in New York City has long been associated with advertising agencies, though all major cities and many smaller ones have important agencies as well. Agencies handle all phases of the advertising business, from doing market research and planning the campaign to hiring models, actors, or musicians, preparing the ads, buying media space or time, and checking on the ads. They compete for advertisers' business by preparing proposals at their own expense and then "pitching" them to clients. The agency the advertiser chooses to work with is usually paid a percentage of the cost of the advertising.

The workroom in an ad agency can look like a playpen for adults. To stimulate creativity, writers, artists, and concept people may lounge on the floor, ride bicycles, or shoot baskets, all the while brainstorming for ideas. While brainstorming, the ad's creators say anything, whatever comes to mind. Most of the ideas are awful, but a few are terrific. And by continuing to brainstorm, one of the awful ideas may be transformed into a gem.

**Activity 5**

Choose an issue that is important in your school right now: improving attendance, supporting a team, recycling paper. In small groups, or as a class, plan a public service ad campaign on this issue. Develop a central concept around which the ads will be designed, brainstorm for a slogan, plan at least five different ads, and create them on poster board. Then arrange to display your ads and try to judge if they are effective.

Getting Started in Mass Media

# Public Relations

**Public relations** (often called **PR**) is a planned effort to foster favorable public opinion. Businesses, political leaders, churches, charities, schools, and other institutions practice PR to influence their own employees, customers, shareholders, neighbors, government agencies, and the general public. Some companies handle their own PR; others hire outside agencies to do the job.

Two kinds of PR that affect the media directly are **press releases** (also called **publicity**) and special kinds of advertising.

A press release looks like a news story, but its purpose goes beyond information. It may report on a speech given by an officer, announce a new product line, or describe the company's outreach program to schools. These reports are sent to newspapers and radio and television stations, which can run them as news—and that means free advertising for the company.

The use of press releases as news sources is controversial. They can provide important, interesting news to readers and viewers. But they can also give institutions with a sophisticated PR staff an unfair advantage over the competition or cover up the organization's less savory activities.

Certain kinds of paid advertising are also PR efforts. An **institutional ad** presents a positive picture of the institution itself. A chemical company, for example, may run an ad describing how it protects the environment.

A **public service ad** is also paid for by the institution, but the message promotes some social good—say no to drugs, prevent forest fires, recycle your throwaways. By sponsoring such worthy messages, the advertiser hopes to mold positive public opinion about itself.

In recent years some institutions have used a third kind of ad in newspapers and magazines: **advertorials,** paid ads that look like news stories or press releases. These ads do include information, but they do so while promoting a specific product or service. An ad for a new drug, for example, may describe the scientific experiments that led to its development.

A similar phenomenon on television is paid programming, or **infomercials,** in which an advertiser buys a program-length block of time to promote a product or service. This program is often presented like a talk show celebrating an "amazing" discovery—an incredible new stain remover or a way to become a millionaire.

**A**ctivity **6**

Look for newspaper stories that probably began as press releases from schools, clubs, businesses, or other institutions. Also find examples of institutional ads, public service ads, and advertorials in newspapers or magazines.

# Criticisms of Advertising

Many consumers dismiss all advertising with a shrug, claiming it doesn't bother them and doesn't affect them. But critics are profoundly disturbed by many aspects of advertising. Some of their more serious criticisms are these:

*Because of advertising, consumerism has replaced other values.* Many people, claim the critics, no longer work to fulfill themselves or to help others, but just so they can buy more things. Too many people see buying as a right. Critics point out that Americans consume more per person than any other nation on earth—and thus contribute more to the depletion of natural resources and to the pollution of air, water, and earth.

*Advertising makes people feel inadequate and leads them to buy unnecessary products or spend more than they can afford.* As you have seen, the image of an ad can play on your fears and make it seem as if personal and social problems will go away if you use certain products. Consumers may say "Of course I know the products aren't magic," but seeing hundreds of thousands of such messages a year may indeed affect people's thinking despite what common sense tells them.

Take society's current attitude toward clothes, for example. Young people want to be accepted, to win the approval of their peers—this desire is perfectly normal. But, some critics claim, advertisers have convinced young people that they will succeed only if they wear high-priced designer clothes and expensive sneakers. Teenagers who accept this reasoning may unfairly reject peers who don't wear the latest fashions, cause family problems by insisting on an expensive wardrobe, work at jobs that take time from their school work so they can afford the clothes, or even resort to theft.

*Advertising contributes to drug abuse.* Since alcohol and tobacco, though legal, cause more personal problems than illegal drugs, many critics object to advertising that promotes the use of these products. But even more worrisome, they say, is the heavy advertising of all kinds of over-the-counter drugs: pain pills, cold remedies, stomach soothers, sleeping pills. Most of the ads show troubled, miserable people who become cheerful, satisfied people after using these medications—though according to medical experts, many of these products are at best unnecessary, at worst dangerous. Of particular concern is the appeal of diet products to teenage girls. According to the critics, the false and dangerous message behind such advertising is that quick chemical solutions will solve almost any problem.

*Advertising takes unfair advantage of children.* When children watch an hour of television, they see about eleven minutes of commercials—for a typical child that amounts to about five hours of commercials a week. But since children are not yet capable of sound judgment, how can they resist the barrage of messages urging them to eat sugary cereal, wear expensive clothes, and buy toys that are spinoffs from the shows? Critics say they can't.

*Advertising is full of false and misleading messages.* Deliberately fraudulent advertising is illegal, but government regulatory agencies can act only after an ad has appeared. Then the process is so time-consuming that often before a complaint can be issued, the offending ad has been replaced by a new campaign.

Sale ads can also be deceptive. True sales exist—end-of-season closeouts, for example, and reduced prices on some items to draw you to the store. But beware of claims like "Comparable value $19.95" and "Special purchase" on items that may or may not be comparable or special. Some forms of sale ads are illegal, such as bait-and-switch advertising. Here a company advertises one item or model at a terrific price—the bait—but then the sales clerk tries to switch you to a more expensive item.

If you believe you have been tricked by an ad, write to your local Better Business Bureau or Chamber of Commerce, your state consumer protection agency, or the Federal Trade Commission in Washington, D.C.

*There is just too much advertising.* No place today is safe from advertising. Besides traditional ads in the major media, direct mail advertising floods into people's homes. Theaters run commercials before the feature film, products appear in the films themselves, schools broadcast news shows that include commercials, lifeguard platforms and trail maps include ads, horse races and tennis tournaments are named after products. The huge number of ads demanding our attention, critics claim, constitutes an invasion of privacy.

**Activity 7**

Each of the following has been suggested as a way to reform advertising. Discuss each proposal. Your teacher may ask you to write a short paper that discusses the pros and cons of one of them.

a. Eliminate all advertising on children's television shows. Networks would still have to broadcast children's shows, but pay for them some other way.

b. Allow radio and television advertising, but group all commercials at the beginning or end of a program.

c. Ban all advertising of liquor and tobacco and limit the advertising of over-the-counter drugs.

d. Ban certain forms of advertising: advertising in schools; billboards; advertising posters on public transportation; commercials shown before a movie in theaters; commercials included with a rental videotape.

# Summary

Advertising helps pay for other media, but it is a major medium itself. Advertisers and public relations specialists do sophisticated research and spend big money to design ads that will appeal to customers. Consumers, therefore, must be very cautious; they must apply sound judgment to both the claim and the image of an ad. There are many serious criticisms of advertising, some of which may lead to new restrictions. But if individual consumers really see and understand the ads, they can start to protect themselves from being manipulated.

# VIEWPOINT

Andrew **A. R**ooney has been called "America's favorite curmudgeon." He has written TV documentaries, books about World War II, and collections of essays. His syndicated column appears in over 250 newspapers, but he is probably best known for his weekly essays on CBS's *Sixty Minutes*. In the essay below, from his collection *Not That You Asked . . .* , Rooney takes the concept of truth in advertising to its logical conclusion.

# **W**here There's Smoke
## Andrew A. Rooney

When the federal jury held the company that made Chesterfield and L&M cigarettes before 1966 partly to blame for the death of Rose Cipollone, it was striking at the very heart of our American way of life.

Rose died of lung cancer at age fifty-eight after smoking a pack and a half a day for more than forty years. The jury ruled that the Liggett Group, which must have been Liggett & Myers tobacco company once upon a time, knew cigarettes were bad for people and should have said so in their advertising. The company was ordered to pay Rose's husband, Antonio Cipollone, $400,000. The award was relatively low because the jury found that the tobacco company wasn't all to blame. It said Rose was 80 percent to blame herself for continuing to smoke after she knew the risk.

That seemed like a pretty reasonable conclusion for a jury to come to. I'm tired of everyone blaming someone else for everything that happens and I was ready to be indignant if the jury laid all the blame on the tobacco company. Anyone would have to be an idiot not to know smoking a pack and a half of cigarettes was bad.

The big news, though, was not who was guilty in this case. The big news was the jury's decision that advertising ought to be honest. Are they crazy?

The lawyer who won the case said the jury concluded the tobacco company was lying in its advertising. He pointed out that one ad for L&M cigarettes claimed they were JUST WHAT THE DOCTOR ORDERED and another for Chesterfields said PLAY SAFE—SMOKE CHESTERFIELDS.

The tobacco industry was pleased that it got only 20 percent of the blame but was nervous because the verdict in this jury case might bring on a flood of lawsuits from people dying of lung cancer.

This isn't what worries me. I'm worried not about the possible decline and fall of the cigarette industry, but about the effect the case will have on the advertising industry itself. Does this mean that in the future ads will have to be honest? Are they kidding? One of the things that makes America great is the unwritten understanding between advertisers and consumers that it's a lot of baloney.

Women know in their hearts that beauty products won't make them beautiful.

Men understand they'll never look like Jim Palmer in Jockey shorts.

We all know foreign countries don't look as exotic as the travel ads picture them.

If advertising has to be absolutely honest, does this mean that GRANDMA'S ORIGINAL HOMEMADE MOLASSES COOKIES would have to be made by Grandma at home?

Can you imagine how ads would read in newspapers or sound on television if they had to tell all? The classifieds would be hard hit:

JOB WANTED: INEXPERIENCED AND UNWILLING TO LEARN, LAZY HIGH SCHOOL DROPOUT LOOKING FOR HIGH PAY FOR LITTLE WORK.

The real estate ads would change:

HOUSE FOR SALE: TWO DRAFTY BEDROOMS AND ONE YOU COULD PUT A COT IN. TWO HALF BATHROOMS. BASEMENT LEAKS, FURNACE ABOUT SHOT. ON WOODED LOT IF YOU CALL TWO TREES A WOODED LOT.

The secondhand-car ads would say something like:

FOR SALE: RUSTY 1981 PONTIAC. SEEN BETTER DAYS. $4,300 OR BEST OFFER OVER $2,000. LOADED WITH GADGETS YOU DON'T NEED. GETS 14 MPG DOWNHILL. FRONT SEAT UNCOMFORTABLE ON LONG DRIVES. MISSING CIGARETTE LIGHTER.

Insurance-company ads wouldn't emphasize how quickly they pay claims. They'd be more like this:

DON'T LOOK FOR YOUR MONEY TOMORROW IF YOU'RE INSURED WITH US. IF WE PAID EVERY CLAIM EVER MADE, WE'D BE OUT OF BUSINESS.

I don't know how many cigarettes the tobacco companies would have sold if they'd had to tell all they knew all these years:

IRRITATE YOUR FRIENDS AND YOUR THROAT, SHORTEN YOUR LIFE, ACQUIRE A FILTHY HABIT. SMOKE UNLUCKY STRIKE CIGARETTES. THEY'RE WORST FOR YOU! ■

## ☞ Your Turn

1. Write a humorous essay about truth in advertising. Use real ads as examples—choose two print ads and two television commercials—and demonstrate how both the claim and the image could be made completely truthful.

2. "One of the things that makes America great is the unwritten understanding between advertisers and consumers that it's a lot of baloney," says Rooney. Write a humorous story about someone who *doesn't* know it's a lot of baloney.

# 3 The News

> **C**ontroversy makes news.
> We don't cause the controversy;
> we just report it.
>
> —Richard Graf

## What Is News?

News is an account of events that interest and concern the public. To you, information about your friend Consuela's flu is news. Students listen to the PA system to get news about club meetings. Community residents want to know about a proposed ball park in town. People all across the state ask who won the governor's race. The whole nation cares about the devastating flood in Ohio, the new space launch, and riots in South Africa.

Information that is newsworthy in one medium, directed to a particular audience, may not be newsworthy in another. Your new kitten may be news to your friends, but that news would not appear in the school paper. The school paper will have news about the Drama Club's new production, but probably nothing about a proposed state insurance law. A fire in an empty warehouse is local news, but a hotel fire that kills dozens of people may make the national news.

Certain qualities help define news:

**Unusualness.** An NBC newsman put it this way: "If an airplane departs on time, it isn't news. If it crashes, regrettably, it is." In a nutshell that comment explains news. News is the different, the unusual, the out-of-the ordinary. People sometimes ask, "Why is the news always bad?" Actually, most of the news media include good news, but the unusual is more often found in bad news. In a way, that's comforting—people living, growing, loving, going about their business is too common to be news. A society in which good news was unusual would be a scary place to live.

**Significance.** Important events, ones that affect many people, are news. Taxes, elections, wars, scientific discoveries, the economy—these are significant in people's lives.

**Timeliness.** Old news isn't news; it's history. People want to hear about the flood while it's happening, not next month when everything has dried out.

**Proximity.** People want to know about nearby events: the asbestos problem in the local school, the new state tax law, the proposed regional highway.

**Prominence.** When well-known people, buildings, or places are involved, that is news. If you are arrested for shoplifting, it might not make even the local news. But if a movie star is arrested, that's news.

**Human interest.** Stories about ordinary people or animals, humorous or dramatic stories, heartwarming or heart-wrenching stories—these often appear in the news because they have human interest, an emotional and personal appeal that draws our attention. Human interest stories are often good news— a minister who runs a drop-in center for troubled teenagers, a veterinarian who specializes in elephants, a sand castle competition.

To be newsworthy a story does not have to have all these qualities, but the more it has, the more newsworthy it will be.

## Activity 1

1. Clip examples of newspaper stories that exhibit each of the news qualities described above. Many stories reflect more than one quality: label them with all that apply.

2. Watch a one-half hour local television news broadcast. Note the subject matter of each story covered and then list the news qualities of each.

3. Discuss the kinds of news stories you enjoy reading or hearing. Why do these interest you? Are there other kinds you think you should pay attention to even if they don't particularly interest you?

## Talking It Over

Tragedy is a media event—but should it be? When there is an earthquake, a serious accident, or a terrible crime, reporters and photographers swarm to the scene. They seek not only to discover the facts, but also to record victims' and witnesses' reactions. Consider recent cases you have read about or seen on television. Then decide which of the following statements reflects your judgment. Discuss your examples and conclusions with your classmates.

■ Tragic stories have a great deal of human interest. Readers and viewers gain compassion for others and appreciation of their own good fortune. The media should report such stories fully.

■ The media act like vultures in the face of tragedy. They violate victims' privacy and turn readers and viewers into voyeurs. The media should show greater restraint in their reporting of tragedy.

Getting Started in Mass Media

# The News Media

Newspapers provide fuller coverage of more stories than the other media, including more human interest and entertainment features. Readers act as their own editors, picking and choosing what they want to read. Newspapers are timely but difficult to store. Some newspapers with national impact are available on microfilm or computer link in major libraries.

News magazines provide in-depth coverage of a number of important stories. They are not quite as timely as newspapers, but they are easier to store; students find them valuable for research on recent events. In addition to the "big three"—*Time, Newsweek,* and *U.S. News & World Report*—there are other, more specialized, news magazines that provide news from a particular political perspective.

Radio news is sometimes called headline news because the reports are usually very limited. Nevertheless, radio is the most timely of all the news media. Within minutes of a disaster, radio listeners know about it. Weather reports are updated hourly. Commuters get up-to-the-minute information about traffic conditions. Radio offers excellent coverage of **fast-breaking** stories, ones that change from moment to moment.

Television news, with the addition of video, provides the most dramatic news coverage. With the power of the camera, viewers can actually see a hurricane raging, soldiers falling in battle, Congress debating an issue, the grisly aftermath of an accident. Television is also very timely although, except for the biggest stories, broadcasters rarely interrupt regular programming to cover the news as it's happening. Reports are confined to regular news programs. Each of the major networks broadcasts news through its local stations, and most local stations broadcast their own news shows, too.

**A**ctivity **2**

1. Take a poll of the class. For each of the news media—newspapers, news magazines, radio, and television—find out how many class members use this medium regularly, occasionally, or never. Discuss your reasons.

2. Choose a news event and compare how the news media handle it. Collect a newspaper and a news magazine account, and tape a radio and television report. What information do you get from each? What is the total effect of each? How does each affect your feeling about the event?

# Where Does News Come From?

Those involved in gathering, organizing, and presenting the news in any medium are **journalists. Reporters**—writers who observe events, interview people, and dig out background information—are the journalists at the heart of the news process. It is up to them to learn of newsworthy events and report on them while the information is still timely. But how do they do this?

Certain places are guaranteed news sources—city hall, the police department, the fire department. A **beat reporter** can be assigned to one of these places; then his or her job is to keep on top of what is happening there. If too many stories are breaking at once, the beat reporter may call for help. The beat reporter must also watch the clock: if a story breaks shortly before the medium's deadline, he or she may have to phone in the report.

A beat can also be a subject specialty. The science reporter regularly checks with research laboratories and teaching hospitals to scout out news. The business reporter follows up on press releases from local firms.

News tips are often phoned or sent in to the media. If the subject doesn't fall within a beat, the editor or producer will send a **general assignment reporter** to cover it. Say a passerby has dramatically rescued a skater who fell through the ice, an anti-pollution rally is being planned, or the circus is requesting a parade permit. A general assignment reporter might be sent to cover events like these.

To cover the almost constant flow of events at important news sources like the state capitol or Washington, D.C., the major media may station a **correspondent,** a reporter who lives and works close to the news source and away from the main office. The media may even maintain a **bureau,** a group of reporters and photographers who cover the source.

Many media also use the services of **stringers,** part-time reporters who watch for news in their area. When a story breaks, the stringer may cover it directly, but if the story is particularly important, the media may send more experienced reporters to follow up.

Besides their own reporters, the major media have another important way to get the news—through the **wire services.** Wire services—also called **press associations**—are independent news gathering organizations that have bureaus, correspondents, and stringers in news centers around the world. Via telephone and satellite links, stories are sent to headquarters and then to the media, where they are received on teletype machines, high-speed printers, or videotapes.

The two major American wire services are United Press International (UPI) and Associated Press (AP). Both sell their services to newspapers and broadcast media, which can run the stories without change, rewrite them, use them as leads for their own reporters, or ignore them. Major media may also subscribe to wire services from other countries—Reuters in England, for example, or Tass in Russia.

In a newspaper you can identify a wire service story by a notation at the beginning of the story. On radio and television, the wire services are not identified, but one study found as much as ninety percent of radio news and seventy percent of network television news (not local news) come from the wire services.

Getting Started in Mass Media

Some major newspapers that have extensive news-gathering facilities also sell stories to other newspapers. The *New York Times,* the *Washington Post,* and the *Boston Globe* are among those that offer such news services.

**Syndicates** are another source of material. A syndicate is a company that contracts with writers, photographers, cartoonists, and others to sell their work to the media. Syndicates seldom supply hard news, but can be a good source of **feature stories,** ones that are entertaining as well as informative.

The media also rely on **press releases** as a news source. As you saw in Chapter 2, various institutions distribute press releases. The media can run these as news, rewrite them, use them as a starting point for another story, or throw them away.

*Activity* **3**

1. In your local newspaper, find examples of local stories that do not include a byline to indicate the author, bylined local stories, and stories from outside news sources such as wire services or syndicates. (Watch for designations like "AP" or "UPI," or tags like "Washington Post News Service" or "King Features Syndicate" at the beginning or end of the story.) Include an example of each in your media log.

2. Which do you think is more important for a journalist? To become an expert in a specialized field, like sports, business, or politics, or to develop critical thinking and communication skills? After you consider this question, write a short report on the qualities of a good journalist.

# Organizing the News

The motto of the *New York Times* is "All the news that's fit to print." More realistically, it might read "All the news that fits in print." Large newspapers with strong advertising support have the money to print more pages than a smaller paper. But printing all the news that pours in locally and from around the world is impossible even for the largest newspaper. One newsman estimated that a typical metropolitan daily receives about 8 million words of copy a day from its staff and news services. Of this, about 100,000 words are published.

The broadcast media are even more limited in what news they can report. Radio broadcasters often devote only five minutes an hour to the news; on television local news and network news usually run half an hour each, and part of this time is advertising. One study found that the script of a half-hour news show, set in newspaper type, filled only three-quarters of the front page of the *New York Times.* Even CNN, the all-news cable network, does not provide twenty-four hours of new programming each day. Instead, it reruns segments throughout the day, intermixed with new reports.

It is usually an editor—the managing editor, the news editor, the news director—who has the final word on what will be printed or broadcast. This person is often called the **gatekeeper,** because he or she controls the flow of news through the gate from the sources to the pages or the screen.

Some stories are so newsworthy there's no doubt they would be included. Reports on a presidential election, a devastating storm, an attack by a serial killer—these will surely appear. But what about the announcement of a new surgical procedure? A minor fire in a bank? If there is room for only one of the stories, it is the gatekeeper's job to choose the more newsworthy.

A large newspaper or broadcast facility may have a number of editors: the city editor (for local news), a business editor, a science editor, a foreign news editor, a sports editor. Senior editors meet each day with the editor-in-chief or producer to lay out pages or time slots. For a newspaper, advertising is blocked first. The number of pages it takes to include all full- or partial-page ads determines the number of total pages for the issue. For the broadcast media, the number of minutes that will be devoted to news or advertising is well established. Once the editors know how much space or time they have to fill, they can decide what news will be used and where or when it will be featured.

## Activity 4

You be the gatekeeper of a school newspaper. Say you have **copy** (written material or illustrations) on the following ten stories, but **news holes** (non-advertising space) for only six of them. Which will you choose? Why?

1. the mid-season resignation of the football coach
2. the announcement of tryouts for the school musical
3. an account of a minor school bus accident that involved no injuries
4. the naming of Rita McDermott and Carlos Montoya as Students of the Month
5. an incident involving vandalism to one of the girls' rest rooms
6. the election of Student Council officers
7. a victory by the field hockey team
8. the announcement of a new, stricter study hall policy
9. the hiring of a new social studies teacher
10. a science class's involvement with a tree-planting project

## Types of News Stories

**Straight news. Straight news** is a factual account of events. It can include opinions expressed by people in the events, properly attributed, but not the reporter's opinion. The writer uses a neutral tone and does not convey approval or disapproval of the subject or the people involved. A reporter who expresses his or her own opinion is guilty of **editorializing.** A reporter may write, "Jacobsen ignored the hecklers and continued her speech." But the reporter would be editorializing if he wrote, "Jacobsen showed great restraint in ignoring the loud-mouthed hecklers."

**Interpretive reports.** Many news events today are so complex that readers and viewers would find "just the facts" confusing. This is especially true of economic trends and scientific discoveries. Most news media, therefore, use **interpretive reports** to help the public understand the news.

Interpretive reports might provide background or project what may happen in the future. They may show how seemingly different events are related. They may analyze the advantages and disadvantages of some course of action. They often include opinions by experts—military analysts, doctors, educators, economists.

In a newspaper, some interpretive reports are labeled "news analysis" or "news interpretation," but others are not. Almost all of the reports in news magazines are interpretive.

Regular television news reports and, to a lesser extent, radio reports may also be interpretive. Television **documentaries** focus on large issues like the problem of the homeless, the history of a war, or the impact of the space program. These shows are expensive to produce and do not garner particularly good ratings, but many critics say television news is at its best when it does this kind of in-depth reporting.

**Investigative reports. Investigative reports** help the media act as the public's **watchdog,** one of the key functions of a free press. The ordinary person has no way of knowing if there is corruption in city hall, secret plotting in the military, or illegal treatment of workers in a factory. Alert reporters, however, may sniff out such problems or may be contacted by **whistle blowers**—people inside the government, the military or the factory who want the problem to be corrected. The famous Watergate story that led to the downfall of the President Richard Nixon's administration was pursued by two *Washington Post* reporters acting on information supplied by a contact they identified only as Deep Throat.

Few radio stations become involved in investigative reporting, but most daily newspapers, local television stations, and the networks have investigative teams. Television news series like *60 Minutes* and *20/20* specialize in investigative reporting, though they may also feature interpretive reports or human interest stories. Some television documentaries rely on investigative reporting.

**Commentary.** Can the media express opinion directly? Yes, if the **commentary** is clearly identified as opinion. All news media can print or air **editorials,** official expressions of opinion. Newspaper editorials appear on the editorial page and are almost never signed. Radio and television editorials are always preceded and followed by announcements such as "This has been a Channel 4 editorial" and are usually read by the station manager or other important executive.

In newspapers and magazines, commentary can also be found in columns and reviews. **Columnists** interpret news events and give their personal opinions about them—sometimes in very strong language. **Reviewers** give critical judgments of artistic efforts: books, movies, plays, concerts, recordings, art exhibits, architecture.

**A**ctivity **5**

1. In a newspaper, find two examples of straight news, interpretive reports, editorials, columns, and reviews. Watch for investigative reports, too, but you may or may not find one. Label each example and include the list in your media log.

2. Find an interpretive report that interests you in one of the news magazines. Be prepared to explain what makes it interpretive.

3. Watch a half-hour local television news show. Note on a chart the subject matter of each report and label each as straight news, interpretive report, investigative report, or commentary. Do the same for a half-hour network news show. Include your chart in your media log.

4. Does investigative reporting have a place in school publications? What would you think about an exposé of student cheating? How would you feel if a reporter had gotten sensitive information from you without telling you it would be included in a controversial report?

# The Question of Slant

News reports are supposed to be honest, accurate, and unbiased. Any journalist guilty of fabricating news or distorting facts is soon fired, but the problem of slant is more difficult. News is **slanted** when it gives a one-sided impression.

Reporters, consciously or unconsciously, can slant news by making it seem as if one side or another is right. Word choice, selection of details, and organization within the story can emphasize some facts or put incidents in a favorable or unfavorable light.

Say there is an accident involving a famous pitcher. "Mack Armstrong escaped unharmed after his car crashed into a tree" gives a different impression than "Mack Armstrong narrowly missed plowing through a group of teenage bicyclists before his car crashed into a tree." Which is more accurate? You would have to know more about the accident to say for sure.

Radio and television news has intensified the problem of slant. Because news reports on these media are so short, reporters watch for dramatic statements or moments—**sound bites.** But taken out of context, these sound bites can give a very misleading impression of a speech or an event.

Editors can also be guilty of slant. In one sense, they are guilty every day because their choice of which stories to print or air gives the public the impression that these are the only newsworthy events that happened—but as you have seen, there is far more news than can be used.

Responsible editors aim for balance. Less responsible ones, however, may focus on government failures and ignore successes (or vice versa), emphasize crime news in a sensational way, deemphasize it so as not to alarm local business, run more stories about a favored political candidate than about the opponent, or give more pages or air time to sports than to the environment.

Editors can slant news in other ways: (1) where they put a story in the paper or broadcast—an "important" murder story on page one, a "routine" murder buried in the paper; (2) how much space or time they give it; (3) how they headline it—"Rioters Storm Concert" vs. "Disturbance Upsets Concert"; and (4) whether or not they include pictures or video. Pictures themselves can slant news, by presenting the subject in a flattering or unflattering way—one candidate caught full-face and smiling, for example, another in partial profile, with eyes out of focus and mouth half open.

News sources, too, can influence the way an event is covered. Government officials and company executives often announce bad news late on Friday—too late for the newspapers or television crews to do anything until Saturday, when there are fewer readers and viewers. Good news, on the other hand, is released in plenty of time for maximum media coverage.

Sources also slant news by creating it. Political candidates and office holders have learned how to use **photo ops**—photo opportunities—to draw the media to places where the politicians can be seen to good advantage. People working for a cause have been known to announce a major rally, call their supporters to come, rally for the few minutes that the reporters and film crews are around, and then disperse.

Most institutions also have **damage control** people, employees who are specially trained to hold press conferences after an event. These employees learn how to deflect embarrassing questions and to get the institution's official explanation across, even if that explanation is incomplete or even untruthful.

*A*ctivity **6**

1. Try to find an example—in the newspaper, in a news magazine, or on television—of a slanted news story or news photograph. Be prepared to explain why you believe it is slanted.

2. Choose an event of interest in the school right now—perhaps the reputation of the football team, or the wisdom of a new policy, or the general condition of the school. Your teacher will divide the class into three groups. Each member of one group will aim to write a straight news story about the event. Members of another group should aim to slant the story positively, and the final group will aim to slant it negatively. Remember: you cannot lie or change the facts.

## Summary

News is an account of anything that interests and concerns people. Unusualness, significance, timeliness, proximity, prominence, and human interest are qualities of news. Reporters, bureaus, wire services, syndicates, and public relations people contribute news to the media—so much news that gatekeepers must pick and choose what to use. Straight news provides factual accounts of people and events, interpretive reports help explain the news, investigative reports expose wrongdoing, and commentary offers opinions. Slanted news gives a one-sided impression of events; writers, editors, and newsmakers themselves can be guilty of slant. Journalism is an honorable profession, but all its practitioners have to hold themselves and their media to high standards of performance.

# VIEWPOINT

**R**ussell **B**aker won a Pulitzer Prize for his autobiography *Growing Up,* describing his childhood during the Depression. He has written a number of other books, including collections of his popular column "Observer," which has appeared in the *New York Times* since 1962. In the essay below, from his collection *The Rescue of Miss Yaskell and Other Pipe Dreams,* Baker uses twists and turns on "dog vs. man" stories to define news.

# Tooth and Man
## Russell Baker

News is made up of a curious variety of events. For example:

1. The rare event: "Man bites dog" is often wrongly cited as the definition of news. Actually, it is the tiniest fraction of the tons of news we consume annually; to wit, a rare event.

2. The daily event: "Dog bites man." This makes up the basic fodder on which the news industry thrives. Since rare events are rare, the industry would collapse if ordinary events—crime, political speeches, child abuse, divorce and massive social and mechanical breakdowns—failed to occur.

3. The unevent: "Dog does not bite man." This is the plot of the news's daily "weather story," which tells us, essentially, "Every day we have some weather, yesterday was no exception, and tomorrow won't be either."

4. The media event: Determined to publicize a cause he thinks is being woefully neglected, man stages a bogus rare event to attract TV and print coverage. If angry about dogs fouling sidewalks, for example, man notifies editors he will bite dog in public thoroughfare in time to make 5 P.M. deadlines.

5. The double media event: Editors tire of covering man biting dog to demonstrate anger about fouled sidewalks. Man tries to tempt editors by offering to bite three dogs. Editors notify S.P.C.A. and rush

reporters and cameras to dog-biting site to get story on irate S.P.C.A. woman biting man for trying to bite dog.

6. The cute event: Dog trained to bark "Ho, ho, ho" is dressed up in Santa Claus duds, placed on plywood throne and photographed not biting news feature writers placed in lap.

7. The annual event: It happens every year, but America never tires of it. We are speaking, of course, of the annual Dog Biting Pageant in Atlantic City. Once again, two-legged finalists with the most astonishing teeth in America compete to determine which, in the judges' opinions, can bite dog with least loss of charm, grace, poise and patriotism.

8. The potential event: The basic headline here is: "Dog May Bite Man." In the most common form, it goes on to say that Senator Glenn or former Vice President Mondale may seek Presidency. The potential event is covered by reporters clustering around dog to hear if he growls dyspeptically at man. If he does, they write, "Dog makes potential man-biting noises," or "Senator Glenn is beginning to sound a lot like a Presidential candidate."

9. The highly conditional potential event: Dog is contented with man, shows no proclivity to bite, but who can tell what he might do if man gave him away and dog ended up in custody of second man? Illustrative news treatment with bipeds: "Senator Robert Dole may seek the Republican Presidential nomination if President Reagan declines to run for a second term."

The all-purpose headline for this story is "Unforeseeable Future Could Change Dog Unforeseeably."

10. The anticipated event: Dog who has never been trained to do anything to man but bite him gains freedom of streets. Newspapers write: "Sharp Rise in Dog-Bitten Men Seen Likely." Or, if the story concerns the political instead of the canine kingdom: "Senator Kennedy Seen as Cinch to Run."

11. The anticipated eventus interruptus: Defying news oracles' predictions that he would bite man after man, dog romps peaceably into park to frolic with kittens and lick man's hand. The headline: "Dog Astonishes Man." What dog has actually astonished, of course, is not man but the news industry, which has covered an anticipated event only to see it turn into an anticipated eventus interruptus, thus supplying a delightful front-page story—"Kennedy Won't Run After All"—where it would have had no story at all had it not covered the anticipated event so thoroughly.

12. La Belle Event Sans Merci: Upon death of dog, man acquires new dog. Sure, old dog never bit man, but who knows what new dog will do? New generation of dogs replacing old generation. What is mood of new dog generation? Should man bite new dog first before dog concludes man is soft and bites man? Should man growl nastily to keep dog polite?

Here we have the skeleton of an important foreign news story, recurrent with each change of government in Moscow. As with the anticipated eventus interruptus—"Kennedy Declines to Run"—it is one of the news industry's favorite events, since it allows for endless fruitless speculation about things that may or may not happen one of these days.

In certain cases news consumers crazed by the merciless onset of such works are tempted to hurl themselves teeth first at the offending news industry. Perhaps they yearn to change the subject by creating a new headline: "Man Bites Man." To elevate their assault from the category of daily event to rare event, they would have to bite at least 20. ■

## ☛ Your Turn

1. Prepare your own list of rare events, daily events, unevents, and so on. Your examples need not all be variations on a theme, as Baker's were. But stick to one subject matter—politics, sports, or music, for example.

2. Choose one of Baker's examples and expand it into a fake news story that satirizes a real one.

# 4 Newspapers

## The Functions of a Newspaper

Newspapers serve four important functions:

- to inform readers about what is happening in the world and their communities

- to influence public opinion through selection of material and commentary on events

- to entertain through interesting stories and features

- to provide the means for local merchants to advertise goods and services

When a newspaper serves these functions well, it becomes an important part of community life. Many people make the newspaper part of their daily routine, reading it with the morning coffee, on the train traveling to or from work, or when they come home from school. Newspaper stories become the subject of daily conversations; some are clipped and saved for years.

Humorist Will Rogers once said, "Take my cat away, take my games away, even my jelly, but leave me my newspaper." In this chapter, you may discover why the newspaper is so important and interesting to so many people.

## Kinds of Newspapers

A newspaper can be classified by its audience and its size.

**National newspapers.** National newspapers carry local news only when those events appeal to a national audience: a major earthquake, a school bus accident that kills a number of children, the opening of an important research laboratory. Examples of national papers are *USA Today,* a general interest newspaper; *The Wall Street Journal,* which excels in business and financial news; and *The Christian Science Monitor,* a widely respected forum of news and opinion.

**Metropolitan dailies.** Newspapers like the *New York Times,* the *Los Angeles Times,* and the *Washington Post* publish several editions a day and reach hundreds of thousands of readers. They serve not only their own cities but the entire region as well. They are often available at newsstands all over the country and even the world.

Such newspapers aim for a balance of international, national, regional, state, and local news, as well as appealing entertainment features. They subscribe to most of the wire services, but they also maintain their own bureaus and correspondents in cities around the world.

**Small and mid-size dailies.** Like the major newspapers, smaller dailies serve their communities with a range of information, but they have little influence beyond their own city. Examples are the Augusta (Ga.) *Chronicle,* the Casper (Wyo.) *Star Tribune,* and the Portland (Maine) *Press Herald.* Mid-size papers vary considerably in quality. Some are very conscientious about covering and investigating local events, but others have only limited staff and fill their pages with material from wire services and syndicates.

**Community weeklies.** Small towns are often served by a weekly or biweekly paper, which emphasizes local news and people. These newspapers generally include no international or national news, and state news only as it affects the community. They usually have small staffs and rely for much of their news on press releases from local clubs, businesses, and government bodies.

**Tabloids.** Tabloids are newspapers printed on paper that measures about half the standard size. Many tabloids are respected newspapers that simply consider this size more convenient for readers. Some tabloids, however, deal in **sensationalism**—an over-emphasis on crime, violence, gossip, scandal, and shock-value stories.

**Special interest newspapers.** Many newspapers serve special interest groups: non-English speakers or members of particular religions, ethnic groups, or organizations. Other newspapers, called **underground** or **alternative** newspapers, present views that differ from those of the establishment (government, business, regular media, and the people that support these established institutions).

**Activity 1**

Collect as many different types of newspapers as you can, either by buying them at a newsstand or bringing in samples from those your familiy subscribes to. Classify each. Then survey each to determine who the audience is and what interests them. Which seem the best newspapers to you?

# The Newspaper Business

In recent decades ownership of newspapers has become consolidated into fewer hands. A number of large **chains,** among them Gannett, Knight-Ridder, and Hearst, own about half of the nation's dailies. And fewer newspapers are published today than at the turn of the century, though the population is much larger. Most cities are served by only one newspaper, which, without competition, may not be motivated to improve. Such newspapers may cut back on local news and investigative reports, which are expensive to gather and prepare, and rely too heavily on the wire services and syndicated material.

**Advertising in the newspaper.** Never forget that a newspaper is a business and is expected to make money for its owners. Some of its income comes from subscriptions, but a greater portion comes from advertising. Advertising depends on circulation, however. The more readers a newspaper has, the more valuable the paper becomes for advertisers who want to reach these readers. Newspapers with larger circulations can attract more advertisers and charge more for their ads. And the more ads and income a paper has, the more pages it can put out.

There are two kinds of ads in newspapers. The majority of ads in the body of the paper come from local retailers, restaurants, and service companies, though national ads may appear. Groups sometimes buy ad space for political purposes, too—ads urging readers to vote for a particular candidate, for example, or write to Congress on some issue. These are called **display ads** and are sold by the column inch, with special rates for quarter-, half-, and full-page ads.

**Classified ads** are smaller, less expensive, and sold by the line. They generally appear at the back of the paper. These are classified—sorted—into help wanted, real estate, automobiles, pets, auctions, household furnishings, and so on.

Few people watch television for the commercials, but some people do buy newspapers for the ads. They look for fashion trends, watch for grocery store sales, check what movies are playing, or look for a job or a dachshund. As you discovered earlier, about 60 percent of the average newspaper is advertising, but this doesn't mean only 40 percent of the paper is useful. Many people find information in the advertising as well as in the news pages.

**Newspaper employees.** The chief officer of a newspaper is the publisher, who may or may not be the owner and who may or may not be involved in day-to-day decisions. The editor-in-chief is in charge of all non-advertising content, while the business manager handles the business end.

Below the editor-in-chief may be a number of section editors, depending on the size of the paper: a wire service editor, a city editor (in charge of local news), a sports editor, a lifestyle editor. Reporters and photographers work under these editors. The copy editor works with the stories submitted by reporters, tightening and improving them and, if necessary, checking facts and correcting grammar. Large newspapers have headline editors who write headlines to fill the space specified by the section editor.

Under the business manager are the advertising sales force, a graphics department that designs ads for some buyers, a circulation department that handles subscriptions, and the production and delivery departments.

**A**ctivity **2**

1. Include labeled samples of display ads (look for a retail ad, a political ad, and a national ad) and classified ads in your media log.
2. Check what categories your local newspaper uses in the classified section. Browse to find jobs you might be interested in some day, a car you might like to own, or some things you might like to buy.

# The Organization of a Newspaper

All but the smallest newspapers are usually organized into sections, but the most important stories always begin on page one. These stories may deal with a variety of subjects—an invasion, a big local crime, a world series victory, the death of a world-renowned person, a major storm, an important medical discovery. The biggest story, called the **lead story,** is usually in the upper right hand corner, where it will catch the readers' eyes first.

Straight news dominates the first section or two of most papers. International, national, regional, state, and local news may be intermixed or divided into subsections.

Following the straight news sections, most newspapers have distinct sections for sports, lifestyle topics, business, and the arts. Some have sections on home and garden, food, science, education, travel, and other topics, though these may not appear every day.

Within each section you will find related news and feature stories and commentary by columnists, who may be local or syndicated. (A syndicate is a company that contracts with writers, cartoonists, and others and sells their work to newspapers all across the country.) The arts section includes reviews of books, movies, television shows, concerts, recordings, art shows, or architecture. These reviews may be written by staff members, other local reviewers, or syndicated writers.

Photographs are very important and usually accompany news stories, feature stories, and press releases. Human interest and artistic photographs—of a child playing in the snow, a man battling an umbrella in a storm, a tree silhouetted against the moon—are also used. Technical improvements have allowed newspapers to use better quality color photographs, which help to snag readers' attention when seen in newsstands.

Newspapers also include death notices and obituaries. A **death notice** is a simple announcement, while an **obituary** summarizes a person's accomplishments and may give details about the death. (You may be interested to know that most major newspapers have a file of obituaries on famous living people! When such a person dies, the research is already done and the newspaper just fills in the information about the death.)

Most newspapers also include **fun features**—comic strips, crossword and other puzzles, astrological forecasts—almost all of which are syndicated. Don't underestimate the importance of fun features—they're often what readers turn to first. One former editor said, "When I worked on a paper, nothing agitated the readers as much as accidentally leaving out the daily horoscope . . . . Nothing printed in the news columns or on the editorial page could compete for impact."

If a newspaper has a Sunday edition, it is always the biggest of the week—more pages, more sections, more news, more advertising. It may also include a magazine section prepared locally, a national magazine like *Parade* or *Family Weekly,* a separate comics section, a television viewers' guide, and special advertising inserts.

*A*ctivity **3**

1. Analyze the organization of your local newspaper. Find out which sections appear daily and which appear some days of the week. If possible, find the average number of pages for each day of the week. If your paper has a Sunday edition, check what sections and what special supplements it includes.

2. Write a short paper about your favorite comic strip. Describe its characters and typical situations. Comment on its message—its view of life—and explain why you like it. Clip and include examples to prove your points.

## The News Story

As you saw in Chapter 2, news stories can be straight news, interpretive reports, or investigative reports. New reporters usually begin with routine straight news, go on to more complex stories, and perhaps graduate to interpretive or investigative work. Routine stories are seldom signed, but more important ones carry the reporter's **byline,** his or her name on the story.

The **dateline,** printed at the beginning of a story, names the story's place of origin. (In the early days of newspapers, when printed news was days or even months old, the dateline included the date of origin.) Many newspapers omit the dateline on local stories.

Reporters must be good observers, good listeners, and good interviewers. They learn to watch for the **5 W's and H** of an event: who, what, where, when, why, and how. The opening paragraph of a news story, called the **lead,** will usually include the answers to most of these key questions. How the rest of the story is organized depends on the subject matter.

**Inverted pyramid style.** In a story organized as an inverted pyramid, the reporter gives the most important information first, the second most important information second, and so on. Diagramed, the story looks like a pyramid standing on its point:

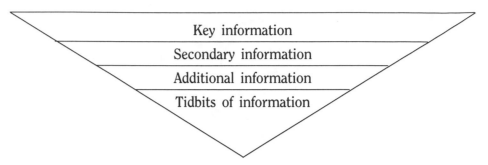

Key information

Secondary information

Additional information

Tidbits of information

This style helps both editors and readers. Editors can cut the bottom paragraph or two to fit a particular space, and readers need only scan the headline and first few paragraphs for the most important facts. Of course, if the subject matter interests them, they can read the whole story.

**Chronological story.** Sometimes chronological order—with events arranged by time—works better for a story. The lead still includes the key information, but then the reporter presents the rest of the details as they happened.

An account of a sports event, for example, often starts with the key information—the winner, the score, and the big plays—and then gives a chronological account of the game. Or a story on a community's weekend celebration opens with a summary of the upcoming festivities and then lists the events in chronological order.

**Composite story.** A composite story combines accounts of two or more events that are linked in some way. The lead usually summarizes the events or shows the connection; then the body of the story can be developed in one of several ways.

Say there were two robberies on the same night following similar patterns. After linking the robberies in the lead, the reporter may tell the details of one in inverted pyramid order, then the details of the second. Or the reporter may go back and forth between the two, giving the most important details first.

*A*ctivity 4

1. Analyze the leads of at least five news stories to see if they answer the who, what, where, when, why and how of the events.

2. Find three examples of news stories written in inverted pyramid style. Be prepared to discuss how many of the lower paragraphs could be cut without sacrificing important information.

3. Find at least one example of a chronological story and one of a composite story.

## Feature Stories

The word *feature* is sometimes used loosely to mean anything in a newspaper that isn't straight news or advertising. More often it refers to a kind of story that is not straight news but is of interest to the public. A feature story is often dramatic or colorful or even humorous, and it is usually strong in human interest. A feature's writing style is often more informal and creative than a straight news story's.

**News features.** Some feature stories are "pegged" to straight news. For example, a newspaper might run a straight news story on gang violence. But a news feature will personalize the story by focusing on one family whose son was killed. The feature will let the family members speak about their lives and their pain. Readers gain not only sympathy for this family, but also deeper understanding of the problem.

**Personality features.** People love reading about other people, so personality profiles have an important place in most newspapers. The profile might be of a famous person—a politician, a musician, or an athlete. It might be about a notable local person—the director of the symphony, a respected school principal, a computer whiz. Or it might be about a relatively unknown person who has done something interesting—a teenager who has opened her own pet care business, a local woodworker who carves ships and puts them in bottles, a woman who found a chest of silver coins in her vegetable garden.

**Travel features.** Since many readers enjoy traveling, feature stories often highlight particular places or ways of getting to them. These stories are frequently written in a chatty style, with the writer combining factual information about what to see, where to stay, and how much it will cost with a personal account of his or her own experiences.

**Help-line features.** Help-lines are a special kind of column in which an expert answers readers' questions. Ann Landers and Dear Abby (the two writers are rival twin sisters) are both syndicated help-line columnists whose personal advice is read by millions. Other columns may answer questions about sports, gardening, or home repair. Some newspapers also have an action line, which tries to solve readers' complaints about businesses or government agencies.

**Miscellaneous features.** Feature stories can be written about almost any subject. A farm that raises llamas? Weird laws still on the books? Long-lost relatives getting back together? What it's like to travel with the circus? Life on a lonely island? A look at school in 1890? The history of cinnamon? All of these and more could become feature stories.

**A**ctivity **5**

In your local newspaper, find examples of each kind of feature for your media log.

# The Editorial Page and Op-Ed Page

Newspapers take their editorial page very seriously. Here is where the newspaper can give perspective to the news and comment on important events. Here is where the newspaper itself can take an open stand and where opposing points of view can be aired.

In smaller newspapers, editorial and op-ed material may appear on the same page, but newspapers typically run this material on a two-page spread. **Editorials** appear on the left, below the newspaper's masthead (which lists its name and publishing information) and represent the official statement of the newspaper's opinion. Editorials may be *interpretive, laudatory* (expressing praise for an individual or group), *critical, persuasive* (such as a recommendation of some course of action or an endorsement of a political candidate), or, occasionally, *humorous* (lighthearted commentary).

Most newspapers also include one or more **editorial cartoons** drawn by their own staff cartoonists or purchased from a news service or syndicate. The subject of the cartoon is sometimes tied to the subject of the lead editorial. **Caricature** and **symbols** are the major techniques used by editorial cartoonists: they exaggerate a public figure's nose or hairdo or smile, or portray a dollar sign on a bag to represent the treasury.

Usually the editorial page includes **letters to the editor,** in which representatives of an institution or ordinary citizens comment on events or prior news stories. Keep in mind if you write a letter to the editor that most newspapers receive far more letters than they can use. Yours is more apt to get into print if you follow the newspaper's guidelines and make your point rationally and clearly. Keep it brief, too. Most newspapers reserve the right to cut your letter.

The page opposite the editorial page, the **op-ed page,** is usually a forum for columnists. **Columnists** are writers whose work appears regularly—say twice a week—under their own names or special column titles. The writers may be staff columnists or syndicated columnists with a national readership. Most newspapers also use guest columns written by experts in a field or by local free-lance writers.

Some op-ed columns provide commentary on current events and hot news issues. A newspaper may choose only those topical columns that reflect its own positions, but more responsible newspapers seek to give readers a variety of viewpoints. Other columns read more like personal essays. One columnist may write about the end of her vacation, for example, and another may humorously mock anyone who enjoys sushi.

**Activity 6**

1. Save the editorials from your local paper for a week and classify each as interpretive, laudatory, critical, persuasive, or humorous.

2. Choose an editorial cartoon that you like and write a short paper explaining the cartoonist's point and the techniques he or she uses.

3. In your media log, list and describe the syndicated, local, and guest columns your paper uses, both op-ed columns and those in other sections. (Authors' names in such columns are usually set in bolder type than a regular byline.)

4. Check your newspaper's guidelines for writing a letter to the editor. Then write one about a recent editorial or news story or about some other issue you think people should understand. If you like, submit your letter to the editor.

# Evaluating a Newspaper

Now that you have studied the news process in general and newspapers in particular, you are in a good position to evaluate any newspaper. As you read, ask yourself how well does this newspaper inform, influence, and entertain the public and advertise goods and services? Does it seem to slant news in a particular direction? Does its commentary offer opposing points of view? Should it include more of a certain kind of news, like news on the environment or on education? Should it have more good news and feature stories? Should it cover more local news?

By considering these questions over several weeks of newspaper reading, you exercise your own critical thinking and can judge how well the newspaper meets your needs and those of the public.

If your local newspaper practices especially good journalism, it may win a **Pulitzer Prize.** Funded by publisher Joseph Pulitzer (1847–1911), these prizes are awarded annually for reporting, commentary, editorial writing and cartooning, photography, and meritorious public service.

**Activity 7**

1. In the average newspaper, the 40 percent of non-advertising space is divided this way: 15 percent wire service material; 10 percent syndicated material; 10 percent in special departments

like sports and lifestyle; and 5 percent local news. Compare the content of your newspaper to these averages.

2. Evaluate your own newspaper overall.

3. In small groups or as a class, design a newspaper just for you. From any newspapers available to you, collect news stories, features, advertising, comic strips—anything you find interesting and worthwhile. Decide how many pages you will need, design a masthead, plan what will go where, and put your newspaper together. Be prepared to explain your choices.

## Summary

From giant national publications to small community weeklies, newspapers exist to inform, influence, and entertain the public and to provide a means of local advertising. They do so through their various departments—news, sports, business, lifestyle. Most news stories are written in inverted pyramid style, with the most important information first, but chronological order and composite stories are also found. Feature stories are more colorful and sometimes humorous. The editorial pages provide a forum for opinion—the newspaper's in editorials and editorial cartoons, and other people's in letters and columns. Newspapers as a business need strong advertising support, which increases as circulation increases.

# VIEWPOINT

**Mike Nichols** has been a reporter for the Fort Worth (Tex.) *Star-Telegram* since 1969, most recently as a columnist. In the following column, from his collection *Life and Other Ways to Kill Time*, he takes a humorous look at the job of a headline writer.

## Go to the Head of the Class
### Mike Nichols

Take a few "attaboys!" or "attagirls!" out of petty cash, dear reader. For you are smarter than you think: You know a second language.

No, your second language is not Chinese or Portuguese, but the shorthand of newspapers—Headlinese. Headlinese is the breath of English with the wind knocked out of it. It is the meat of communication with the fat fried away. It is the skeleton of syntax with the soft, supple, yielding flesh torn . . . oh, you get the idea.

You grew up with "heads." Deciphering their telescoped message is second nature to you now. You've come to accept the present tense for past events. You've learned to do without modifiers. You can survive for days without an auxiliary verb.

(Children of the fifties got a head start by listening to Hollywood Indians talk in westerns. "Braves ride far, take many scalps." "Senate cuts tax bill, hikes aid plan." Paleface reader see heap big similarity?)

Here is a little known fact: The people who write the stories usually are not the people who write the heads for those stories. No, heads are usually written by copy editors. Copy editors are an unsung, disciplined, intense subspecies. They can reduce any human thought, emotion or action to five words or less.

Their minds are a precision instrument—a shoehorn.

They think in monosyllables. Two copy editors passing in the hall: "Hi," "'Lo." "How do?" "Good. You?" "Fine." "Bye." "S'long."

In Headlinese, space is at a premium. So smaller is better. Thus "compete" becomes "vie." "Consider" becomes "eye." "Connection" becomes "tie." And should Princess Diana compete for the chance to consider a connection: "Di to vie to eye a tie."

Sigh.

Yes, dear reader, you can read headlines. But how would you like to learn to *write* headlines? Amaze your pals! Amuse your colleagues! Abuse your ulcer! Neat-o, eh? All right. First, shut yourself into a phone booth. Then put your head in a lunch box. Then put the lunch box in a vise. *Now* you are in the proper frame of mind.

So let's try one. Remember Hamlet's soliloquy? Eloquent, to say the least. No, to say the *least,* we'll reduce those 276 words to a headline. A three-word headline. Find your old copy of *Hamlet* (it's under that short table leg in your dining room) and review that time-honored passage:

"...that is the question...slings and arrows...there's the rub... mumblemumble...mortal coil...mumblemumble..."

What is Shakespeare saying? Well, Hamlet is considering killing himself to escape the torments of life. But he then wonders if the unknown torments *after* life might not be even worse. And he realizes that he has thought too much about it to be able to take his own life. Besides, he wouldn't want to miss the annual office Christmas party, when his uncle—the evil Claudius—always drinks too much mead and wants Hamlet to help him sing "My Buddy."

Now squeeze those several thoughts into one basic thought. Think short.

"Prince
rejects
suicide."

Not bad. Squeeze still more. Think stubby.

"Dane
picks
life."

Better. Come on—squeeze just once more. Think *stump* (kids, do not attempt this headline at home without adult supervision).

"He
to
be."

There! You did it! Just like ol' Will woulda. For a first effort, that was satisfactory. Make that "acceptable." No, make that "decent." No, better make that "good." Better yet, make that "OK."

Say, has anybody out there got a shorter word for "OK"? ∎

## ☛ Your Turn

1. Each student should bring in a newspaper story with the original headline cut off. Exchange stories. Then, working in pairs, follow Nichols' advice and write headlines that are accurate and yet highly condensed.

2. Write an essay modeled on Nichols' essay. Choose a passage from a novel or play. First quote the passage and summarize it in several sentences. Then reduce the essential point to a sentence, then to a phrase, then to a shorter phrase, as far as you can go.

# 5 Magazines

## The Role of Magazines

No matter what your interests, there are magazines to fit them. Do you enjoy rock music? Take a look at *Song Hits* magazine. Personal computers? Try *PC Computing.* Coin collecting? See *The Coin Enthusiast's Journal.* Do you care about the environment? Try *Garbage.* Dream of exotic places? Browse through *Travel & Leisure.* Are you looking for religious inspiration? Try *Guideposts Magazine.* Considering moving to Vermont? Check out *Vermont Life Magazine.*

If you visit a newsstand, you might be dizzied by how many magazines there are to choose from, yet these are only a small portion of the three thousand or so that are directed to the general public and only a tiny fraction of the 20,000 magazines published in the United States. These magazines range from tiny, home-produced journals that reach a few hundred readers to giants that reach millions. Hundreds of new magazines are launched each year.

Why this surge? Because magazines meet the needs of both readers and advertisers. Readers can find magazines that exactly fit their interests, and advertisers can reach a market that is likely to be interested in their products.

Furthermore, magazines are relatively easy to start up. Unlike newspapers, which usually own their own printing equipment, most magazines hire out the printing. **Desktop publishing**—programs that allow even home computers to turn out professional looking text and graphics—make start-up even cheaper.

But hundreds of magazines also go out of business every year. Unless a magazine is well-conceived and gains loyal readers and satisfied advertisers quickly, the cost of production will soon eat up the initial investment. Even well-established magazines can die after losing readers or advertisers to other markets. By the time you read this book, some of the magazines mentioned here may already be out of business.

The purpose of magazines is the same as that of newspapers: to inform, influence, and entertain the public and to provide a means for targeted advertising. With a few exceptions, however, magazines seek a niche among readers rather than the broad group that newspapers aim for.

**Activity 1**

Survey the class's magazine readership. Have each member list all the magazines he or she reads regularly; then have a small group tally these responses. Discuss why you like or dislike certain magazines.

# Kinds of Magazines

Reviewers vary in how they classify magazines; the groups below are based roughly on content.

**General interest magazines.** General interest magazines aim for the widest possible audience, though not necessarily the biggest. They usually include something for everyone—lifestyle trends, food, outdoor activities, poignancy, humor. They emphasize people and personality over issues and ideas, and use informal, nontechnical language.

The giant in the field is *Reader's Digest,* with upwards of 16 million readers. If you scan the articles and ads in *Reader's Digest,* you will find it is geared to a middle-of-the-road audience with traditional values rooted in family life and patriotism. National Sunday supplement magazines, purchased and distributed by newspapers, also reach millions of readers each week.

Some smaller magazines, published by companies and associations for their customers or members, can also be classed as general interest. *Ford Times,* for Ford owners and others, is an example. Many of the in-flight magazines, like *Aboard* and *USAir Magazine,* also aim to please a wide range of people, with some emphasis on the business traveler.

**Mass group magazines.** Many magazines are targeted to either males or females, or to a particular age or ethnic group. *Scholastic Scope,* for example, appeals to high school students of both sexes, but *Sassy* is geared to girls and *Boys' Life* to boys. Mass group magazines emphasize how to do something (be more beautiful, bake a pie), how to spend time (go camping, take a trip), and how "special" people live (stars and ordinary people who have accomplished something). They also offer an escape from everyday life (through both fiction and articles).

Among children's magazines are *Humpty Dumpty's Magazine* for very young children and *Ranger Rick,* for children interested in nature and natural science. Children's magazines are a growing field; some are spin-offs from movies and toys, like *Teenage Mutant Ninja Turtles* and *Barbie,* but others have more promise, like *Sports Illustrated for Kids,* geared to ages eight and up, and *Young Consumers,* the youth version of *Consumer Reports.*

Women's magazines range from *Family Circle,* written primarily for young homemakers; to *Savvy,* for working women; to *Glamour,* which appeals to sophisticated women—or women who want to be sophisticated.

For men there are sports magazines like *Field and Stream,* how-to magazines like *The Family Handyman,* and sophisticated magazines like *Esquire.* You might be interested to know that more women read men's magazines than vice versa. A magazine like *Sports Illustrated* is read by many women, but even so, the majority of articles and ads are geared to men.

*Modern Maturity,* with circulation close to 20 million, is geared to older men and women. *Ebony* aims at black readers—and reaches close to 10 million of them.

**News and opinion magazines.** As you saw in Chapter 2, the three biggest news magazines—*Time, Newsweek,* and *U.S. News & World Report*—concentrate on interpretive reports of important world and national events. Others in this category provide political perspective. *National Review,* for example, is a respected conservative magazine, and the *New Republic* is an important liberal publication.

**Quality magazines.** Some magazines look for readers who are sophisticated, well-educated, and reasonably prosperous. Among the most successful of these is *National Geographic,* with upwards of 10 million readers. Many families collect this magazine for years; others scout out old copies in flea markets. Also in this category are magazines of literary merit like *The New Yorker* and *Atlantic Monthly,* which specialize in high-quality fiction, poetry, and commentary on modern life, mostly by well-known authors.

**Fiction magazines.** The number of magazines that specialize in fiction has declined in recent decades. Most of those that remain are **genre magazines** that concentrate on a particular kind of fiction—romance, mystery, horror, or science fiction. Among these magazines are *Modern Romances, Ellery Queen's Mystery Magazine,* and *Isaac Asimov's Science Fiction Magazine.*

**Special interest magazines.** While all magazines target their contents to a particular audience, special interest magazines define that audience very narrowly. Readership ranges from a few thousand to a million or so, but few of these publications exceed that. The following list is limited; many more magazines are published within each category, and many more categories could be included.

| | |
|---|---|
| Hobbies and crafts | *The Workbasket, Postcard Collector* |
| Photography | *Popular Photography, Outdoor Photographer* |
| Nature | *American Forests, National Wildlife* |
| Parenting | *Parents Magazine, Baby Talk Magazine* |
| Food | *Bon Appetit, Chocolatier* |
| Health | *Prevention, Health* |
| Gardening | *Modern Horticulture, Flower & Garden* |
| Pets | *Bird Talk, Dog Fancy* |
| Entertainment | *TV Guide, Soap Opera Digest* |
| Personal finance | *Money, Consumer's Digest* |
| Military | *Marine Corps Gazette, Military Review* |
| Games and puzzles | *Dragon Magazine, Chess Life* |
| Science | *Omni, Popular Science* |

| | |
|---|---|
| History | *American Heritage, Wild West* |
| Disabilities | *Arthritis Today, A Positive Approach* |
| Cars and motorcycles | *Car and Driver, American Motorcyclist* |
| Ethnic interest | *American Dane, The Jewish Monthly* |
| Travel | *Travel and Leisure, Vista/USA* |
| Regional | *Dallas Life Magazine, Montana Magazine* |
| Humor | *Mad Magazine, National Lampoon* |

**Literary magazines.** Literary magazines provide a showcase for established and new writers of literary essays, stories, poetry, and reviews. They are often called "little" magazines because their circulation is very small, ranging from a few hundred to a few thousand. Many of these magazines are associated with universities—like *The Denver Quarterly* published at the University of Denver. Others, like *Ploughshares,* are independently published.

**Trade magazines and professional journals.** Trade magazines are geared to members of a particular trade or profession. Truckers, bricklayers, farmers, government workers, jewelers, machinists, painters, the toy industry—all these and more have magazines devoted to their interests. Scientific and other professional journals (the word **journal** is often used to distinguish these publications from commercial publications) provide information about new research to biologists, astronomers, doctors, lawyers, historians, linguists, and other professional groups.

1. As a class, purchase, borrow from the library, or bring from home as many different magazines as possible. Browse through them, and classify each in one of the categories above. Record your list in your media log.

2. If you have two or more magazines in the same category— say, two or more music magazines—compare and contrast them. How are they alike? How are they different? Are they actual competitors, or do they appeal to slightly different audiences? Which do you think is the better magazine?

# Comic Books

Comic books are one form of magazine geared exclusively to entertainment. About 300 million are sold each year, to children *and* adults. Though some people criticize comics, their defenders passionately support them. Devoted readers save every issue. Collectors—up to 100,000 of them—scour flea markets, attend conventions, and pay big money for early or rare editions.

A wide variety of comic books are published. There are some featuring funny animals like Donald Duck and Heathcliff, funny people like Archie and Richie Rich, and fantasy characters like Caspar and Wonder Woman. There are martial arts comics, romance comics, horror comics, and more.

Getting Started in Mass Media

*Classics Illustrated* is a special kind of comic book that adapts famous books to comic book form. Many a student has failed a literature test by relying on *Classics Illustrated* instead of reading the book, but many readers, too, have been inspired to read the book after reading the *Classics Illustrated* version.

Most comic books originate with free-lance writers, who propose ideas based on series characters or independent stories. Once an outline has been accepted, the writer provides a script for the artist, or an artist draws the story and then the writer supplies captions and dialogue.

**Activity 3**

1. Obtain a *Classics Illustrated* comic of a book most of the class has read and compare the two versions. What events have been omitted? How faithful to the book's descriptions are the artist's visualizations?

2. Examine a number of comic books and newspaper comic strips. What techniques do cartoonists use to convey loud voices? whispers? thoughts? odd noises? surprise? inspiration? fear? swearing?

3. Team up the artists and writers in the class and come up with a proposal for a comic book, either for an existing series or one based on an original idea. Produce a few panels for the book.

## A Magazine Profile

A **magazine profile** is a description of the content of the magazine and its **demographics**—who its readers are, their gender, age, marital and job status, religion, income, spending habits. This profile is used in two ways.

First, the profile defines the magazine's mission—what it seeks to offer to readers. *Americana* magazine, for example, links traditional values and nostalgic topics to today. Thus, you might find articles on wood carving, a visit to an old New England village, or the perfect blueberry muffin, but you will not find articles on industrial robots or new fashion designs.

Second, the profile is used to attract advertisers, who can then buy and target their ads appropriately. Rolls Royce and Mercedes Benz, for example, are more apt to advertise in *The New Yorker,* with its upscale audience; Ford and Chevrolet will advertise station wagons in family magazines like *Reader's Digest.* And a sneaker company that advertises in men's, women's, and teen magazines will use different models and different layouts in each.

**Activity 4**

1. Choose a magazine from those the class collected in Activity 2 and prepare a profile of the magazine based on the editorial and advertising content. For each magazine, prepare a chart that answers the following questions:

a. What is the title, the date of the issue you surveyed, the number of pages, and the cover price?

b. Is the magazine illustrated with photographs? drawings? cartoons? Are the illustrations in black-and-white, color, or both?

c. List the subject of each magazine's feature (main) article (for example, personality profile of star, how to improve in school).

d. List the subject matter of each shorter article (for example, roundup of money tips, two movie reviews).

e. Does the magazine include fiction and poetry? If so, describe what kind of stories and poems.

f. How many pages of ads are included? What percent of the total is this?

g. List the kinds of products advertised in the magazine, and how many ads for each category appear (for example, six car ads, three travel ads).

Based on this information, write a paragraph profiling the magazine. Overall, what is its mission? Who are the readers? What is the typical editorial (non-advertising) content? What kinds of ads does it run?

2. Do the same with your favorite magazine. Then write another paragraph answering this question: Does this magazine provide information, influence, entertainment, and advertising that realistically matches your life? Or does it present an ideal world, one you would like to be part of? Explain your judgment.

3. Post and survey the charts the class prepared in exercise 1. Now be the media buyer. If you were the manufacturer, in which magazine(s) would you buy space to advertise a camping tent? a candy bar? an inexpensive computer? an expensive camera? a new line of blouses? a middle-priced resort? lo-cal frozen food? a dictionary? elegant grandfather clocks? contact lenses? In each case, be prepared to explain your choice(s).

# The Magazine Article

As you have seen, newspaper stories are basically factual. Only editorial writers, columnists, and reviewers directly express their own opinions. Magazines, too, can include editorials, columns, and reviews. Some also run opinion forums in which different writers give the pros and cons of an issue—whether teenagers should hold jobs during the school year, for example.

A magazine feature article, however, may be a strictly factual account of a topic, or it may be closer to an essay in which the writer espouses a particular point of view. As a critical reader, you must recognize when a writer is expressing opinion and judge how well he or she supports it.

Like the reports you write in school, magazine articles are built around a **controlling idea,** usually stated very near the beginning of the article. The controlling idea identifies not only the topic, but the point the author wants to make. The author of one article about a teenage tennis star, for example, may concentrate on what a well-rounded person the champ is. Another may stress how much dedication and work went into becoming an expert. A third might evaluate the star's chances in an upcoming tournament.

The opening of a magazine article is called the lead, as in a news story. Instead of providing the most important information first, however, a magazine lead tries to get the reader's attention, perhaps with statistics or a dramatic quotation, perhaps with a moving anecdote, perhaps by asking a challenging question.

Then the article is organized with a beginning, middle, and end, rather than in the inverted pyramid style of a newspaper story. The author develops the controlling idea with details, facts, reasons, examples, anecdotes, and expert opinion.

Relevant information that is interesting but not crucial to the controlling idea is often presented in a special section called a **sidebar.** The article on the tennis ace, for example, might include a sidebar that lists the star's major victories or the diet she follows.

The style of writing must match the magazine's profile. A magazine of nostalgia, for example, would not describe in technical terms the function of an old mill, though it might recount in warm, colorful tones the history of an old mill that has become a charming restaurant.

*A*ctivity **5**

1. Find a magazine article you believe is basically factual. Identify the controlling idea. Then list and provide an example of each technique the author uses to develop this idea.

2. Now find an article you believe expresses an author's opinion. (Do not choose an editorial, a column, or a review.) Again identify the controlling idea and the techniques the author uses to develop it. Now evaluate the essay: Did it convince you?

3. Find articles on the same or similar topics in two or more magazines. Compare the controlling idea, the development, and the style of the articles. How does each fit the magazine's profile?

# Magazine Production

The staff of most magazines is much smaller than that of a newspaper reaching the same number of people. Heading up the magazine is the editor-in-chief or, occasionally, the publisher (who is usually the owner or a representative of the owner). On large magazines there may be other editors—a fiction editor, fashion editor, or music editor, for example.

To plan editorial content, editors will work from a formula that fits their magazine's profile. Each edition includes certain kinds of material in predetermined amounts—perhaps one short story, one sports article, two fashion articles, an advice column, and three feature articles. The editors plan each issue at an editorial conference, usually months before the magazine is printed. They discuss the focus of that issue, article and photo ideas, and proposed layouts.

Where does the content come from? Some of the articles may be staff produced, with writers and photographers sent to do a story on, say, a popular band or the wonders of Charleston. Some material is assigned to writers known to the magazine, either by reputation or through their past work for the magazine. And some comes from free-lance writers who submit ideas or manuscripts to the magazine.

Free-lance article writers usually **query** the magazine first—that is, they write a letter describing the proposed article and showing how it fits the magazine's profile. If the editors like the idea, they will give the writer the go-ahead on **spec** (speculation): they may accept or reject the article when it is written.

Writers of essays, fiction, and some nonfiction articles (especially very timely ones) usually submit the complete manuscript. Magazines refer to these unsolicited (unasked for) manuscripts as the **slush pile** or **over-the-transom** manuscripts—from the days when poor writers who couldn't afford postage would push their manuscripts through the transoms above older-style office doors. The big magazines are deluged with unsolicited manuscripts, very few of which get published. Every year, however, some do, and this is a time-honored way for young writers to make a start.

**A**ctivity **6**

Design a magazine that would be perfect for you. Use the chart outline in Activity 4, but answer each question in terms of your ideal magazine. You may want to go a step further and produce an issue by culling articles, illustrations, and ads from existing magazines. Then you must decide on the magazine's size, design a cover, and lay out what goes where in the magazine.

# The Magazine Business

Like newspapers, many magazines are owned by chains. Time, Inc., and the Hearst Group are two. Some critics worry that corporate ownership will adversely affect magazines' editorial policy and cause them to become more bland.

**Income.** At most magazines, income depends on circulation—subscription and newsstand sales—and advertising, with advertising being more important. Ad rates depend on circulation, but advertisers are willing to pay a premium to reach their target audience. Even though *Sports Illustrated* has higher ad rates than *High Fidelity,* a sneaker ad is apt to be far more effective in *Sports Illustrated.*

In recent years, as cable has opened new television markets, magazines' and newspapers' share of advertising dollars has declined. The result may be greater dependence by these media on circulation income. To increase newsstand sales, some magazines make deals with retailers to ensure a good display, and almost all aim for colorful, appealing covers that will catch the attention of browsers.

**The effect of advertising.** On the one hand, highly successful magazines with solid readership can afford to be choosy about advertisers. *Modern Maturity,* aimed at older readers, will not accept ads for wheelchairs or hearing aids or any ad with the words "pain, inflammation, suffer, hurt, ache, and flareup." *Architectural Digest* and *Bon Appetit* refuse pet food ads. The upscale fashion magazine *Mirabella* does not accept ads from "ordinary" cosmetic and clothes companies.

On the other hand, some magazines work closely with advertisers and tie their editorial content to the ads. A travel magazine, for example, may include feature articles about resorts that buy ads. Articles in many magazines include brand names and information about where to buy the products. Some magazines accept the advertorials you read about in Chapter 2—ads that look like articles.

What is worrisome is that many advertisers want a "supportive environment" in the magazine. That means that they do not want to see articles about controversial issues or ideas. As one critic put it, they want the magazine to view its audience not "as readers who happen to consume but as consumers who happen to read."

Because advertisers have punished magazines that pursue an independent editorial policy by pulling their ad dollars, some magazines have become more cautious about what they print and, say critics, less interesting and worthwhile.

This trend may accelerate as competition for ad dollars increases. Those magazines that keep a sense of mission and refuse to cater to advertisers could end up with fewer advertising dollars. Some magazines will try to fight by raising the cover price, but whether readers remain loyal and pay the increase remains to be seen.

## Activity 7

1. Reexamine the magazine you profiled in Activity 4. Are there any articles that tie in directly to advertising? By contrast, are there any articles that might offend potential advertisers?

2. Consider your favorite magazines. Would you classify each as a magazine that sees you as a reader who happens to consume, or as a consumer who happens to read?

## Talking It Over

Traditionally, magazines have pursued both money and mission: they want to succeed in business, but they also have an editorial vision they want to share with readers. The pressures discussed above, however, may make a sense of mission difficult to carry out. How do you think the reading public will react? Decide which of the following statements reflects your opinion. Be prepared to discuss your reasons.

■ Magazines should maintain a sense of mission, not worry about advertisers, and if necessary, raise their cover price to remain profitable. I think readers would be willing to pay more for meatier content and less advertising.

■ Magazines are already expensive, and I doubt that readers will be willing to pay much more. Magazines must tailor their contents to what advertisers are willing to pay for. Magazines can be interesting without being controversial.

## Summary

There are magazines to fit every reader interest and need—some 20,000 of them in all, 3,000 directed to the general public. A few of these are general interest magazines that appeal to a wide range of people, but most appeal to more limited groups—teens or men or music lovers or horse owners. A magazine profile provides a snapshot of the magazine—its contents and its readers. Advertisers use this information to target their ads, and the magazine staff uses it to determine the content of each issue. That content comes from assignments to staff members, regular contributors, and other free-lance writers. Most magazine income derives from advertising, and this has led to some worry about whether magazines can retain a sense of mission to their readers.

**J**ohn **W**ood began writing when he was in the fifth grade and has continued ever since. He has tried his hand at novels, sportswriting, travel writing, screen writing, and comedy writing. Today he is senior editor of *Modern Maturity* magazine and continues freelancing. In this essay Wood deals humorously with the complications of magazine writing.

# Editors Who Leave Too Much (And the Writers Who Sell to Them)

## John Wood

Just when you've squeezed your foot in the door at *Aluminum Siding Illustrated,* Joe Editor—who's bought most of the fillers you've sent his way and just offered you the cover story for the next issue— jumps ship to become editor at *Cat Breeding Gazette.*

You have three choices: 1) start all over again at *ASI* by introducing yourself to its new editor; 2) scratch *ASI* as a potential market altogether; 3) follow your cat with a camcorder the next time she leaves the house.

Your best bet is Number 3. Joe is your cash cow, an editor who loves your work. The problem is that adjusting to Joe's new magazine could prove more harrowing than replacing his gold star in your Rolodex. So many magazines merge, are sold, developed or dropped these days that the road an upwardly mobile editor travels is filled with potholes of indecision, hairpin mood swings and career detours.

To illustrate, we'll follow Mary, a typical writer, who sends a query to her favorite editor, Joe, at *Arizona Highways.*

"Joe!" Mary gasps over the phone. (Always sound breathless when speaking to an editor.) "Have I got a thousand words for you on 'hiking in the pueblos'! Trekking among Tecumseh's ghosts, scouting ancient ruins by moccasin—"

"Tecumseh never was in Arizona."

"Geronimo then," she improvises. "The winds rushing through the canyons sound like Indians chanting . . . it's a natural."

"Okay, 750 words," Joe says. "And hurry."

Mary knocks out the story in two weeks—and it comes back before she's home from the post office. Clipped to it is a form rejection letter. Mary calls *Highways:* Joe no longer works there. Curious, she calls him at home.

"*People Magazine.*"

"Joe?"

"Oh sorry, didn't I tell you? *Highways* had a housecleaning; I'm now Southwest correspondent for *People*."

"Congratulations. You always do land on your feet." After some small talk (editors love small talk; it makes them think you like them), Mary gets to the point: "Any place for my hiking piece there?"

"Actually, that's not a bad idea," he says. "But this is *People*. Kill the pueblos, cut it to 200 words, hype a local Indian, and give it a head with some puns."

She redoes the piece, sends it in. A month goes by with no reply. His phone is disconnected. *People* tells her Joe quit after two weeks and moved to Kansas City to write jokes for Hallmark cards.

At Hallmark, Joe is as upbeat as ever. "Bet you thought I forgot about your Indian chief," he says. "I didn't—you're experiencing deja vu. Ha-hah! Get it? That's our newest birthday line. Listen, I think I can help you—somebody has to. Ha-hah! But seriously, trash the chief and give me some Pocahontas one-liners for Thanksgiving."

"Gee, I don't know," Mary says. "From pueblos to Plymouth Rock is quite a jump." But she sends in a batch anyway. A month later—to her surprise—a check arrives. Elated, she calls Hallmark.

"Joe?" a secretary says. "He left us last week."

"But he seemed perfect for the job."

"Are you kidding? You should have seen the Pocahontas joke he just bought. That was the last straw."

Mary calls Joe at his new home, and is relieved to hear there are no hard feelings—especially since Joe's just been hired by McGraw-Hill in New York to run its children's book division.

"Still love your Pocahontas idea," he says. "Just juvenilize it and it'll be swell. Something like *How John Smith Almost Lost His Head* or *The Adventure of the Pilgrim and the Squaw*."

Wiser now, Mary calls the new office before sending her story in. "He ran out last month," Joe's replacement tells her. "Said he wanted to climb a mountain and wrestle a grizzly."

On a hunch, Mary calls *Outside* in Chicago and asks for Joe. Sure enough, he picks up the phone. "This is where it's at, Mary! Your Indian love story could work here—but you gotta add some danger. Make it first-person, take along your boyfriend and do something perilous. Reenact the Sun Ceremony, track scorpions barefooted—we'll pay medical expenses."

Thirty days, 5,000 words and a broken engagement later, Mary calls Joe to proclaim her victory over the elements and her breakup with her fiancé—who left her stranded in the mountains after three prairie dogs poked their noses into the tent the first night. But Joe no longer works there.

"Hey, I got an offer I couldn't refuse," Joe says when Mary catches up to him at his new *Playboy* penthouse office. Before she knows it, they're discussing a Squaws of the Southwest layout—when his intercom buzzes.

"Gotta go, hon. Hef needs a sixth for Monopoly. Call me tomorrow."

She does: "Forget *Playboy*," Joe says, "my screenplay was optioned! Spielberg loves it. Sly wants it. I'll be in Hollywood tomorrow—let's do appetizers and have a look at your treatment, say, threeish—"

"Enough!" Mary jumps to her feet. "I've done this idea to death. How'll I know you won't be copyediting in Cleveland by *threeish* tomorrow?"

"You don't, doll, that's the thrill. One day you're a star, the next you're doing *Hollywood Squares* with Anson Williams."

Mary hates *Hollywood Squares*. She delivers a manuscript to Joe's office by 2:30 the next day. For three months he doesn't return her calls. Finally, the treatment comes back in a torn manilla envelope.

She calls Joe's office—Ted the Tattooist answers. She calls his Beverly Hills duplex—Jessica Hahn answers. She calls the long-scratched-out original number on her Rolodex—Joe answers, sounding like Tom Waits after a bad night.

"I'm out of a job," he rasps. "No where else to go. I'll have to f-fr-free-free-lance. Never thought I'd stoop so low."

"Any luck so far?" Mary asks, trying not to gloat.

"Just one. Sold a quickie to *Arizona Highways* on pueblo ruins. Idea's been kicking around in my head for months. Don't know where it came from."

Mary gasps.

"And you know what?" Joe says. "They liked it so much they asked me back. Will you send me that Pocahontas query again? It'll work there this time—but you'd have to redo it."

You know she will. ■

## ☛ Your Turn

1. Choose a silly idea for a magazine article—say, the joy of peas or the body language of dogs. Now describe how you would slant your article for five different magazines mentioned in this chapter.

2. John Wood's imaginary editor does a stint at a greeting cards company, a medium whose products are used for personal communication. Design and write a greeting card of your own—sentimental, humorous, sympathetic—for some occasion. Then, if you like, send your card to a friend or relative.

# 6 Books

## The Role of Books

Helen Keller, blind and deaf from an early age, gained the gift of language with the help of a dedicated teacher. She had this to say about books: "No barrier of the senses shuts me out from the sweet, gracious discourse [conversation] of my book friends. They talk to me without embarrassment or awkwardness."

Millions of people feel as Keller did, that books are their friends, speaking to them of magic worlds, bold ideas, astonishing facts, quiet memories, helpful hints, and worthy causes.

Books are crucial in modern life, a driving force in education, business, law, science, medicine, and entertainment. Through books, students gain the legacy of knowledge earned by those who came before. Business leaders share their methods. Lawyers, scientists, and doctors keep up with new developments. People of all ages find information, pleasure, relaxation, and inspiration.

Books, newspapers, and magazines share a common heritage, the invention of movable type in 1456. Before this time, books were laboriously handcopied and quantities were necessarily limited. But the new printing processes opened the door to mass communication—and to universal education and far more rapid flow of ideas.

The presses have not stopped since. Before 1500 Europe was producing about one thousand titles a year. By the mid-1960s, worldwide, the output was closer to one thousand titles a day.

Books lack the immediacy of other mass media, but they make up for that by greater thoroughness and permanence. Books are saved and treasured, in great public libraries and in personal collections. Readers go back to favorite books, rereading them again and again. Others enjoy a book once and pass it on, wanting others to share their discoveries.

There is concern in society that television has lured some younger people away from books. Those who have already discovered the joy of books, however, are hooked for life. And as others become aware of the vast array of books available, they too will find that unrivaled knowledge and pleasure await them between the covers of books.

**Activity 1**

List the last five books you have read, not counting textbooks. (You may, however, include books you read as a class assignment—a novel in English class, perhaps, or a book on the planets for science class.) Write a brief paragraph about each book: Tell what it is about in a sentence or two; rate it as poor, average, good, or excellent; and explain your rating.

# Types of Books: Fiction, Poetry, and Drama

**Fiction**—stories about made-up characters and events—accounts for less than 10,000 of the 50,000 or so titles published in the United States each year. Fiction gives so many readers such a rich reading experience that it looms larger in their minds than it does is in the publishing world.

**Youth books.** The toddlers-to-teens market has grown enormously in recent years. Much of it has been fueled by status-conscious parents and grandparents, but young people, too, are begging librarians for certain titles and buying their own books in stores and through book clubs aimed at kids. Superstar authors—like Chris Van Allsburg and Maurice Sendak among children's authors, and Cynthia Voight and Richard Peck among young adult writers—command huge audiences. Over 300 book stores in this country specialize in children's books.

In years past, the number of novels written with teenage protagonists and targeted to teenage readers was limited. In recent years, however, YA (young adult) books have multiplied—and generated controversy. Some authors, like Robert Cormier and Judy Blume, do not flinch from stories about cruelty, death, divorce, mental illness, and sexuality—topics that some people believe are not appropriate for young people. Defenders say that YA novels should tackle these issues because they are part of teenagers' real-life experiences.

**Genre fiction.** Like the genre magazines, genre books tell particular kinds of stories. **Science fiction,** like Ray Bradbury's *The Martian Chronicles,* explores space and time travel, parallel universes, and advances in science and technology. **Fantasy,** like **J.R.R. Tolkien's** *The Hobbit,* tells stories of magic and strange creatures and adventurous human beings. **Horror** novels, like Stephen King's *It,* delve into monsters and the dark side of human nature. In **mysteries,** like Agatha Christie's *The Orient Express,* an amateur or professional detective solves a crime. In **romances,** like Judith Michael's *Deceptions,* the heroine finds love. (**Gothic romances** always include a heroine in danger, a mysterious man, and a shadowy mansion—all inspired by Charlotte Bronte's 1847 novel *Jane Eyre,* still widely read.)

**Popular fiction.** Most genre fiction is read by a core of devoted fans, but some, like Richard Adams's animal fantasy *Watership Down* and almost any horror story by Stephen King, cross over into popular fiction—novels published for general readership. Popular fiction includes thrillers like Peter Benchley's *Jaws,* historical novels like James Clavell's *Shogun,* and nostalgic portraits like Garrison Keillor's *Lake Wobegon Days.*

Both genre fiction and popular fiction offer readers escape to a world that may seem more fascinating than the real world. The best of both types, however, also offer something more—complex characters, rich settings, clever plots, a glimpse of history, a struggle over important issues or ideas. A recent example is *Clan of the Cave Bear,* by Jean Auel, the story of a young Cro-Magnon girl brought up by a Neanderthal tribe.

Much popular fiction, however, relies on a formula: Love conquers all; Work hard and success will be yours; Goodness will be rewarded and evil punished. Nothing is wrong with these formulas as light entertainment, but readers should realize that meatier fare is available.

**Literature.** Defining the difference between popular fiction and literature is difficult. One test is time; if a book is still read decades after it was written, it's apt to be classed as literature. Readers today still enjoy books like the *Odyssey,* the epic adventure tale written by Homer in the ninth century B.C.; the *Arabian Nights' Tales,* which includes "Ali Baba and the Forty Thieves," dating back to about 1450; and *A Christmas Carol,* written by Charles Dickens in 1843.

Another test is seriousness of purpose. Does the author want simply to entertain, or does he or she want to explore a serious aspect of human life? E.M. Hall's 1921 novel *The Sheik* (a best-seller that became even more famous as a silent movie starring Rudolph Valentino) falls into the first category, while John Steinbeck's 1947 novel *The Pearl* falls into the second—and as a consequence is often included in literary anthologies for students. This test can be tricky, however. In the first place, even an author with a serious purpose must tell a compelling story; otherwise, he or she might as well write an essay. In the second place, authors can use humor or fantasy to serious purpose, as Ken Kesey does in *One Flew over the Cuckoo's Nest* or George Orwell does in *Animal Farm.*

A third test is the reaction of reviewers and critics in both the popular press and literary journals. In their columns, expert readers evaluate the worth of new books—but they are not infallible. Reviewers in 1851 were not kind to Herman Melville's *Moby Dick,* but that book is today considered a giant of American literature.

**Drama and poetry.** Only about a thousand plays and collections of poems are published each year in the United States. Plays are usually judged only when they are produced, but newspapers and magazines occasionally review poetry.

**Humor.** It's hard to know how to categorize humor books, which are popular sellers every year. Collections of insults, jokes, or cartoons (like *Calvin and Hobbes,* by Bill Watterson) are often given as gifts—but usually the gift-giver reads them first, being careful not to crack the binding!

**Activity 2**

1. List the novels recorded by class members in Activity 1 and categorize each as YA, genre fiction (be specific), popular fiction, or literature.

2. Find and read several book reviews of fiction in your local newspaper or in a magazine. Then summarize each reviewer's judgment: Does the book have literary merit? entertainment value? little merit at all? Also summarize the reviewer's criteria—standards of judgment.

3. Divide the class into "fan clubs" for the various genre. Each group should prepare a short oral defense of that genre, explaining in more detail the kinds of stories these are and why readers like them. Back up your claims with reference to specific books; if possible, bring copies of the books to class for your presentation.

# Types of Books: Nonfiction

**Nonfiction** books—those rooted in fact—account for the vast majority of books published each year. Publishers, librarians, and book stores differ as to how to categorize nonfiction, but you may find the following division helpful.

**How-to and self-help books.** How-to books tell readers how to do something—make friends, play baseball, fix motors, use a word processor, stay healthy. These books are extremely popular, in both hardcover and paperback editions, and often remain top sellers for years. *How to Win Friends and Influence People,* written by Dale Carnegie in 1936, is among the all-time best-selling books in paperback—by mid-1989 more than seventeen million copies had been sold. Travel, cooking, and gardening books are so popular that most bookstores have special sections for each of these categories.

**Biographies and autobiographies.** In a biography, an author tells the story of another person's life. In an autobiography, the author tells the story of his or her own life. Autobiographies of stars and super-athletes sell well, but you'll frequently see "With So-and-So" listed under the star's name as author. Usually in these cases, "So-and-So" did far more writing than the star. Even when the only name listed is the star's, the book may have been written by a **ghost writer** who agreed to remain unnamed.

**Fields of study.** Every field of study—history, science, psychology, sociology, business, politics, economics, religion, sports—yields new books each year. These books may be textbooks directed to students, **trade books** intended for the general public (like Edith Hamilton's *Mythology*), or professional books written for practitioners in a field.

**General nonfiction.** Some nonfiction books are like extended versions of a newspaper or magazine article. Piers Paul Read's *Alive,* for example, is the true account of how the survivors of a plane crash in the Andes continued to survive—through cannibalism. And Alex Haley's *Roots* is the saga of the author's family, from its origins in Africa to today.

Other nonfiction books are collections of essays, short writings that combine fact and opinion. Humorous collections, like Erma Bombeck's *The Grass is Always Greener over the Septic Tank* and Bill Cosby's *Fatherhood,* are especially popular. Other books are almost like extended essays, often rooted in personal experiences or social observation. Recent examples include *The Cat Who Came for Christmas,* by Cleveland Amory, and *All I Really Need to Know I Learned in Kindergarten,* by Robert Fulghum.

**Reference books.** Reference materials like dictionaries, thesauruses, atlases, books of quotations, and almanacs are an important group of nonfiction books. Some, like encyclopedias, are purchased primarily by libraries, but others are best-sellers with the general public year after year.

**A**ctivity **3**

Browse through your school or public library to find a number of nonfiction books you think you might find interesting. Choose a variety of books—a how-to book, a biography or autobiography, a book related to some field of study, a general nonfiction book. Base your choices on the subject, the title, the information you find on the book jacket, and the table of contents. In your media log, record the title, author, and date of publication of each book. Then in a sentence or two identify the subject of the book and why you think you might find it interesting.

# Book Publishing

How does a book get into print? All books start with an idea, either from a writer or an editor. If the idea comes from the editor, he or she will seek out an author who can do the job. If the idea comes from a beginning novelist, he or she will usually complete the book before seeking a publisher. Established novelists and most nonfiction writers, however, often get a commitment from a publisher before completing the manuscript. In either case the writer usually submits a summary, an outline, and sample chapters to the publisher, directly or through a literary agent.

A **literary agent** acts as an author's representative in negotiations with the publishing company. For this service, the agent usually receives a 10 or 15 percent fee based on the author's earnings. Book publishers, like magazines, are flooded with unsolicited manuscripts, few of which are accepted. Publishers pay more attention to proposals from agents because the agents are careful to submit only appropriate manuscripts. An agent would not make the mistake, for example, of submitting a book on dog training to a publisher that specializes in science fiction and fantasy.

Once the idea is accepted by a publisher, the editor works closely with the writer and the production department. Sales and publicity departments work on promotion—listing the book in a catalog, advertising it, arranging exhibits at conventions, supplying review copies, and visiting book stores and schools. Some authors help promote their books by appearing on radio or television talk shows or by visiting book stores for autograph sessions.

Books issued first in hardback often come out later in paperback. Some publishers have also introduced lines of original paperbacks, like Bantam Books' Spectra line of fantasy books and Loveswept line of romances. A title can also be sold to book clubs that offer members less expensive editions.

**Self-publishing** and **subsidy publishing** are two other routes to getting a book into print. In both cases the author pays for the printing and advertising of the book, but in self-publishing the author acts as his or her own publisher while established companies offer subsidy services. Computer desktop publishing programs have made self-publishing easier, but most of these books are not big sellers. Subsidy publishers are often called the **vanity press** because usually the only return the author receives is the pleasure of seeing his or her name in print.

In traditional publishing, the author is paid a **royalty**—a percentage of the price of each book sold. Most authors are given an **advance** on the royalties when they sign a contract or complete a manuscript.

Publishing houses range from very small companies like Appalachian Mountain Club Books that publish a handful of books a year to giants like Houghton-Mifflin that publish hundreds. Like other media, book publishers are being bought up by bigger book publishers or by conglomerates.

But unlike other media, book publishers make money only in sales. As the number of smaller publishers dwindles, critics worry: Will profit-oriented publishers hold onto a sense of mission, seeking out good books even if they won't be giant sellers? Or will they tend to limit their offerings to books that are sure to be commercially successful?

## Activity 4

Publishing houses work with artists as well as writers—artists who design the book and its cover and provide illustrations or photographs. Examine a number of hardcover book jackets to see how they are organized. Now design a new jacket for one of the books you listed in Activity 1 or for a book you are reading now. Use a large piece of construction paper, folded correctly. Include the title, author, and publisher on the front cover and the spine. Illustrate the cover. Write a **blurb**—a description of the book that will spark readers' interest—and type or print it neatly on the front flap. Continue the blurb on the back flap. On the back cover you may use another blurb, a teasing excerpt from the book, or snippets of made-up reviews.

# Best Sellers and Prize Winners

The big blockbuster novel that everybody's talking about this year and that sells millions of copies is definitely the exception in publishing. In fact, only a tiny percentage of books achieve this success, and only a small number of writers make the huge six-figure advances you sometimes read about in the paper.

How does a book become a best seller? The pull of a big name author is one way. A new horror story by Stephen King or a romance by Judith Krantz is almost guaranteed to become a best seller. To become a big name, however, a writer must start with a wildly popular first or second book. Advertising and promotion play a big role in spurring sales of first novels. Some books are ideally timed to catch reader interest. In her 1990 autobiography *Now You Know,* Kitty Dukakis describes her battle with addiction to alcohol and pills. Published a year after her husband Michael lost the Presidential election and at a time when interest in alcoholism was high, the book became an almost instant best seller.

Best-sellers lists may not precisely reflect the nationwide popularity of a book or its quality, however. The national lists published in *The New York Times Review of Books* and elsewhere are based on sales estimates from a few large bookstores. Best-sellers lists can be fun because they can give clues to the public's interests, but many fine books never make the list. Choosing a book that's on the list will give you something to talk about with a lot of people, but don't reject a book just because it's not a best seller.

Winning an award can help a book's sales, though it doesn't guarantee best-seller status. Two important American awards are the National Book Awards and the Pulitzer Prize. **National Book Awards** are given for fiction and non-fiction. The **Pulitzer Prize** is most associated with journalism, but awards are also given for fiction, drama, poetry, history, biography or autobiography, and general nonfiction. (You might be interested to know that one YA book has won the Pulitzer—*The Yearling,* by Marjorie Kinnan Rawlings.)

Various genre prizes are also awarded each year—the **Edgar** to mysteries and the **Hugo** and the **Nebula** to science fiction, for example. The **Newberry Medal** is awarded to the author of an outstanding book for children or young adults, and the **Caldecott Medal** is given for outstanding children's book illustration.

The highest international literary prize is the **Nobel Prize,** which is awarded in recognition of a body of work rather than for an individual book. American writers who have won the Nobel Prize, from earliest to most recent, are Sinclair Lewis, Eugene O'Neill, Pearl Buck, William Faulkner, Ernest Hemingway, John Steinbeck, Saul Bellow, Isaac Bashevis Singer, Czeslaw Milosz, and Joseph Brodsky.

## Activity 5

1. Get a copy of the local best-sellers list from your daily newspaper or a bookstore. Some newspapers include brief comments on what each book is about. If yours doesn't, delegate a class member to check with a librarian or bookstore. Discuss the books. Why do you think each book has become a best seller? Which seem interesting to class members?

2. Choose a book you have read recently that you believe deserves to become a best seller. Now write a glowing review that will help the book's sales.

## Talking It Over

Students often grumble that any assigned book immediately loses its appeal, but most are proud of themselves when they finish it. What books should be assigned, however, is a matter of hot debate in educational circles. Think about the books you have read as assignments and those you pick for yourself. Then decide which of the following statements reflects your judgment. Discuss your reasons and examples with your classmates.

■ Books of proven literary worth should be the backbone of the curriculum. Reading these books broadens students' taste and allows them to share a common culture.

■ Relevant contemporary books should be assigned to students. More students will complete the assignment, and more will be turned on to the joy of reading.

## Summary

Books are among the most enduring of the mass media. Some people save them for years, and libraries save them for centuries. Fiction, which accounts for about one-fifth of the books published, includes youth books, genre fiction, popular fiction, and humor. Drama and poetry account for an even smaller share. Of all these books, only a few endure as literature. Nonfiction primarily offers information—how to do something, accounts of real people's lives, understanding in a field of study, reflections on life. An idea for a book can come from a writer or an editor. The two then work closely together until the book is published. Best-selling books are the most talked about books published each year, but they may not win important prizes or endure as literature.

# VIEWPOINT

**Bruce McCabe** is a feature writer for the *Boston Globe* and an amused observer of the literary scene. Alive to modern timesaving techniques, he nevertheless pokes gentle fun at those people who look to machines to achieve greatness.

## Now You Can Just Slide in the Disc and Watch the Plot Thicken

### Bruce McCabe

For as long as I can remember, I've wanted to write a great book. I'd settle for a great movie.

Just as I get rolling on my idea, though, it comes out as someone else's creation. It turns out that someone else had the idea and executed it before I did.

Until I met Tom Sawyer—a television writer-producer of the short-lived CBS series "The Law & Harry McGraw" and creative writing teacher at UCLA—I had assumed that originality was my problem. I just wasn't original enough.

Sawyer, whom I recently interviewed in Boston, gently broke the news to me that originality is a dead issue. "It's all been done," he said, shaking his head sympathetically.

He was in Boston to talk about a new interactive computer program he co-created (with Arthur Weingarten, another writer-producer) for, as he put it, "wannabe" fiction writers like me.

His program is called Plots Unlimited.

"It's an idea machine. It has a data base of 2,000 plot fragments," Sawyer said in the naturally hyperbolic way writer-producers talk. "Each is linked to from two to 14 other plot fragments. You can build a story tree-like with 200,000 possibilities. They cover every aspect of human relationships . . . "

He paused.

". . . except incest."

Plots Unlimited shows how you can build your own variations on exemplary hits of all forms: Movie ("Casablanca"), play ("Death of a Salesman"), novel ("The Great Gatsby"), TV series ("I Love Lucy") and story (Hemingway's "The Short Happy Life of Francis Macomber" and Robert Louis Stevenson's "Dr. Jekyll & Mr. Hyde").

Plots' cost is $399, which might seem pricey unless you consider that it could be your investment in a goldmine like the new "Gone With the Wind," novel or movie, your choice.

The way Sawyer describes it, once I program my computer with Plots Unlimited, I'll never have to worry again about what they always told me I had to worry about—what Sawyer called "the writer's age-old nemesis, the problem of integrating character, conflict and structure."

It's all been done for me. All I have to do is change a few wrinkles.

After being pumped up by Sawyer, I decided to bounce his theories off a more traditional writer and teacher from Cambridge, a more traditional literary community than LA.

I called Karen McQuillan, a mystery writer ("Deadly Safari") and teacher of courses in plotting and writing mysteries at the Cambridge Center for Adult Education.

Although she had never investigated literary computer creativity, she indicated she probably never would. In fact, she seemed appalled by the very idea.

"Imagination is an organic process harnessing the unconscious. The flow can be slow and messy. You work it out yourself. It's not mechanical," she said.

"Writing is also terribly personal," she said. "It involves memories, things you've forgotten, fantasies. It's mysterious. I don't know how you'd nail it down."

I hung up.

I don't, either. ■

## ☞ Your Turn

1. Ideas can generate ideas. Try this. One student writes a beginning paragraph for a story. Then that student passes the beginning paragraph to another student, who writes a second paragraph. And the second student passes it along to a third, until everyone has had the chance to add to the story. Each student must follow up on what was done before, but may add new elements. (Warning: the story may not be complete with one go-around of the class, but it should be, well, kind of fun.)

2. Write a brief essay or story that is a humorous variation of a book you have read or a television program you watched.

# 7 Television

## The Role of Television

Television has been called the "massiest" of the mass media—for good reason. Ninety-eight percent of all American households own at least one television set; almost two-thirds of them have two or more sets. Of the 90 million households in the country, 80 million watched President Bush's speech about the beginning of war in the Persian Gulf; 50 million watched the final "M*A*S*H" episode in 1983; 40 million have watched the Super Bowl in recent years; 30 million watched the television premiere of the film *Gone With the Wind* in 1976; 20 million watched the Beatles in their first American television appearance on the *Ed Sullivan Show* in 1964. Sixteen million households watch the typical sitcom, or situation comedy, and 10 million watch the typical information show.

Statistics about individual viewing are no less astounding. The average person watches four hours of television per day; the average household watches seven hours. The average kindergartner has already watched more hours of television than he or she will need to spend to earn a college degree. By age twelve the average child has watched 13,000 hours of television—a year and a half of his or her life. In a lifetime the average person spends nine years in front of the set.

Small wonder that television is the most controversial of the media. Critics call it the boob tube and the idiot box; defenders call it a window on the world, a magic carpet of discovery. Critics say it promotes mindless viewing of mindless programs; defenders claim it enlarges both knowledge and understanding. Critics say it stifles creativity and promotes distorted thinking; defenders say it encourages a new way of thinking and a consciousness of the global village—one world, with interlocking hopes, needs, and problems.

Social observers often urge parents not to use television as an electronic baby-sitter. They suggest all viewers use the off button much more frequently. Neither is likely to happen, however. Outside of a few individuals and families, Americans will continue their love affair with television. That makes it even more important to understand this medium and to be aware of its strengths and weaknesses.

**A**ctivity **1**

1. According to the Department of Education, the average eighth-grader spends 21.4 hours per week watching TV, 5.6 hours on homework, and 1.8 hours on outside reading. Use the chart in your media log (Chapter 1, Activity 1) and compare your personal statistics to these figures. If your figures are above or below the average, try to analyze why.

2. Think about your family's TV habits. Are they typical? Is the TV on during mealtimes? As a family activity, how does TV watching rank with other activities like going to movies, visiting friends, playing sports or games, reading, or just talking?

3. Newspapers routinely run articles about television. As you work with this chapter, watch for announcements, reviews, commentary, and reports on ratings. Include these in your media log.

## Networks and Stations

The three major networks—CBS (Columbia Broadcasting System), NBC (National Broadcasting Company), and ABC (American Broadcasting Company)—still dominate television, though cable TV is beginning to challenge them. Each network produces programs—news and live events—and buys programs from others.

The networks buy a majority of their programs from movie studios, independent producers, and syndicates. (Like syndicates that supply newspapers, TV syndicates provide shows, both new programs and reruns.) These companies first prepare **pilots** of proposed programs—sample episodes that the networks can judge themselves, show to prospective advertisers, or run experimentally in the off-season.

The networks also set the broadcast schedule—what will be aired when. Sometimes they base these decisions on **compatible programming**—a block of similar programs intended to keep viewers hooked. And sometimes they use **counterprogramming**—offering something very different from another network. In the fall of 1990, CBS applied both principles when it scheduled the popular *Murphy Brown* and *Designing Women* along with a new entry, *Rosie O'Neill,* in the 9 to 11 P.M. slot. This schedule was designed to snag female viewers and to run against ABC's *Monday Night Football.*

The law allows each network to own five VHF and two UHF stations and **affiliate** (associate) with other stations. Each network has about two hundred affiliates. The networks send programs to affiliates via special telephone lines. An affiliate need not broadcast every network program it receives, but in practice affiliates seldom reject programs.

Except for the stations owned by the networks, affiliates are independently owned and managed businesses, just like newspapers, magazines, or book publishers—and like them are often owned by giant corporations. The number of TV stations in an area, however, is limited to the number of signals that can be broadcast. The **FCC** (Federal Communications Commission) decides who can have access to these signals. Anyone wishing to open a TV station must obtain a license from the FCC.

A station's license must be renewed every three years. In theory, each station must prove that it is serving the public interest by the variety of its offerings—network and local programs, educational and entertainment programs, sports and public affairs. In recent years the renewal process has been made much easier, however, and in practice few stations have lost their licenses.

Sixty percent of the schedule of most affiliates is network material, 15 percent is produced locally, and 25 percent is bought from syndicates and other suppliers.

A fourth network, Fox, has in recent years made a dent in the viewership of the Big Three. It, too, owns seven stations and is affiliated with more than 125 others. FCC rules forbid the Big Three from owning shows directly but do not place this restriction on newcomers like Fox, which can produce any number of hours of programming a week. The Big Three claim this exception gives Fox (and, potentially, other newcomers) a competitive edge and so are seeking changes in the FCC rules.

PBS (Public Broadcasting System) is the only noncommercial network in the country; it too has about two hundred local affiliates. It was created by the Corporation for Public Broadcasting, established by Congress in 1967 specifically to provide educational programming. PBS programs come from its own affiliates, independent producers, and international sources like the BBC (British Broadcasting Company).

**Activity 2**

1. Using the newspaper or a TV viewing guide, make a chart in your media log that gives the channel number, call letters, and network affiliation, if any, of each local station.

2. Now list the programs that each station produces locally. Start with the viewing guide, but you may need to check programs you're not sure about by watching them. Next to each program, tell what kind of program it is—news, local interest, religious, sports, or whatever.

# VHF, UHF, and Cable

Regular television broadcasting is carried on **VHF** (very high frequency) and **UHF** (ultra high frequency) signals. VHF stations operate on channels 2–13, which can reach a 50 to 100 mile radius. UHF stations, operating on channels 14 to 83, reach a smaller area. Cable programs are not really broadcast at all, but sent via the cable itself on channel numbers assigned by the cable company.

Cable TV was originally conceived as a way to extend TV reception to areas distant from broadcasting facilities, but it turned out to have much greater potential. The large number of clear channels that cable can carry means it can offer a wide variety of programming—channels that specialize in news, sports, music, the arts, children's programs, education, vintage movies, even shopping. Because each channel targets a relatively small audience, cable service is sometimes called "narrowcasting." Cable got a boost in 1991; viewers signed up by the thousands to watch CNN's live coverage of the Gulf War.

Broadcast television is free for anyone with a TV set; cable is not. Subscribers pay varying monthly fees for basic service (local stations only), expanded service (a package of additional channels, like The Nostalgia Channel and Arts & Entertainment), and premium channels (channels with separate fees, like Home Box Office and The Disney Channel).

Cable's reach is growing—by 1990, 60 percent of American households had cable service—but its full potential has not yet been tapped. Many of the non-network channels have indeed offered quality alternatives to the networks. The Discovery Channel, for example, offers a number of fine nature, cultural, and travel programs, and Nickelodeon has been praised for its imaginative children's programming. Other channels, however, offer only reruns or uninspiring movies. True, premium movie channels offer new films without commercial interruptions, but sports fans in some areas are angry that events once seen free on local stations are now available only through the pay sports channel.

Consumers have also been annoyed by poor service in some areas and by rising prices. Local governments grant licenses to cable companies but after that have little control over them.

One service every cable company must provide is a community access channel and the facilities for residents to use it. Results have been mixed. Some communities are televising local government proceedings, local sports events, school plays and musical productions, and special shows produced by both students and adults. Other communities, hindered by a lack of local leadership or interest or an unhelpful cable company, have made little use of community access channels.

**Activity 3**

1. If your community receives cable, post a chart of the channels it offers. Indicate on the chart which channels are in the basic and expanded packages and which are premium channels. Delegate one class member to find out the cost of installation and monthly service. Ask people you know how they would rate the service and the cost.

2. Discuss the community access channel in your community. Delegate a committee to visit the studio to find out what facilities and help are available and what local programming is currently aired. Discuss the quality and the interest level of local programming.

# TV as a Storyteller

Just as with books, most TV programs can be classified as fiction or nonfiction. The amount of fiction viewed by most Americans on TV far outweighs what they find in books. Indeed, as one analyst said, "Television's greatest power is in its role as the central storyteller for the culture."

Most television fiction comes through series built around an established cast of characters. In recent years sitcoms have dominated the lists of most popular programs. Sitcoms can revolve around traditional families with father, mother, and children (*The Cosby Show*), nontraditional families with a single parent or guardian (*Kate and Allie*), lifestyles (*The Golden Girls*), or the workplace (*Night Court*).

Series other than sitcoms have a more serious tone, though they may include humor. A high percentage of these are built around law and order—police, private detectives, lawyers, or mystery writers who solve crimes. Another group focuses on professional groups—what life's "really" like among lawyers, doctors, or some other occupation. Other series are developed around family life or lifestyles, like *Life Goes On* and *thirtysomething.*

A third kind of series is the anthology, like the old *Twilight Zone,* which uses a different cast and story each week.

Though there are some series that are admired by all but the most die-hard critics, it is fiction specials that often get the highest marks. Many made-for-TV movies and mini-series, both comedy and serious drama, are run-of-the-mill, but others demonstrate TV's power to entertain and move. The ABC mini-series *Roots* dramatically explored the black experience in America, and the CBS production of Arthur Miller's play *Death of a Salesman* shows TV's ability to bring serious drama to the screen.

**Docudramas** based on true stories (the word comes from *documentary* plus *drama*) have been especially popular in recent years. Other dramatic specials use a fictional story to explore a current issue, like homelessness, AIDS, or prejudice.

And in considering television fiction, you mustn't forget soap operas—called operas because of their involved plots and soaps because the first of them, broadcast on radio, were sponsored by soap companies. Critics and fans alike laugh at the soaps for being melodramatic and silly—but the fans, millions of them, continue to watch.

The main character of most soaps is a woman (the majority of viewers are women) for whom viewers feel empathy—sympathy and kinship. She and the other characters face a host of problems, most of which end up solved. The viewers want their programs to take an optimistic view of life. And one thing is sure: these characters are not lonely and bored. To lonely, bored viewers, those TV lives look fascinating.

**Activity 4**

1. List your three favorite current TV series and your three favorite reruns. Have one class member tabulate the votes to find the class favorites. Discuss why you like these shows.

2. In an almanac or another source, find a list of the most recent Emmy and ACE winners. (**Emmies** are awards in various categories given annually by the Academy of Television Arts and Sciences. **ACE's**—Awards for Cable Excellence—are the cable version.) Do you agree with the choices?

3. Identify serious issues that have been used in recent TV series or fiction specials. How effective was the treatment of the issue? Did you learn anything from the show? If the issue was a controversial one, did the show present just one side or more than one?

## The Message of Television Fiction

Television fiction, except for a few topnotch series and specials, is the subject of intense criticism—though sometimes, when the industry has attempted to meet these criticisms, a new crop of critics has sprung up to complain about the solution.

One of the reasons for these problems is the sheer quantity of time that must be filled. Some analysts doubt that there is enough writing and production talent to fill all those hours with quality programming.

A second reason is financial. Before the networks can please viewers, they must first please the advertisers who pay for it all. Advertisers want to be assured of reasonably happy viewers who will be receptive to the sales messages. And they do not want to spark controversy. Groups with one complaint or another against some show have organized boycotts and letter-writing campaigns against its advertisers. Quite often, however, if the advertiser pulls out, it is then deluged with complaints from those who like the show! Bland, predictable shows let advertisers avoid this dilemma.

**Plastic smiles and happy endings.** In most television series, comedy or not, everything turns out rosy. Dad and daughter fight about her curfew? Never mind—they'll be smiling at each other within half an hour. A corpse is found and all clues point to the hero-detective? Never mind—within an hour he'll make fools of those who accuse him and have the real murderer tied up, ready for the police to haul away. In real life, problems seldom go away so quickly, but the ease with which they're solved on TV leads viewers to develop distorted expectations, say critics.

And oh, how sweetly people solve those problems! A mother may get angry—but within moments she cools off and hugs her child. A young man may have a serious gripe against his girlfriend—but very soon they're sitting quietly, talking it over, kissing and making up. People on TV don't scream at the top of their lungs. They don't hold a grudge for weeks or months. They don't strike out at those who've hurt them. They don't cry alone—for long. On TV, someone who is sad or worried always has a relative or friend who brings cheer and comfort. On TV, no one is lonely.

When series step out of these formulas, however, they face criticism from the other direction. The highly acclaimed *Hill Street Blues* featured an overworked police department, a poverty-ridden neighborhood, dedicated people and truly corrupt ones, and problems that didn't go away. It was criticized in some circles as depressing. The top-rated comedy series *Roseanne* focused on the members of a middle-class family who worry about money, take out their grievances on one another, trade insults freely, and yet manage to love one another. This show has been criticized as vulgar. The occasional *After School Special* features serious problems of young people—peer pressure, pregnancy, suicide, alcoholism—and has been criticized for being too realistic.

Programs that tackle such issues owe a debt to Norman Lear, who changed television forever when he introduced *All in the Family*—a sitcom with a social conscience. Though many people were (and are—the show is still very popular in syndication) offended by Archie Bunker himself and the issues the show used in its plots, most see the show as superior satire, using intolerance to point the way to tolerance and good will. Should people tuning in to a comedy find a serious message, too? Lear's answer was, "I don't know another way to create theater every week except to deal with those situations I find important in human values."

**Stereotypes and standards.** A stereotype is an oversimplified picture of a group of people, as if this picture were true of all the members of the group. At one time all blacks on television were maids or porters. All gangsters were Italians in heavy coats and slouch hats. Hispanics—when they appeared at all—were stupid, and Orientals were sneaky. The Irish were lushes, and Russians were dangerous.

The main characters of most series were WASPs—white Anglo-Saxon Protestants—whose biggest worries were crab grass and falling cakes. Families never had money worries. Moms stayed home, wore heels as they cleaned house, and baked cookies at least once a week. Dads worked hard—in offices—but didn't bring office problems home with them. Children shared their toys and looked adorable at bedtime. The family played games and staged their own talent shows—but they never watched TV.

You have probably realized by now that these stereotypes have by no means disappeared from TV. Yet some progress has been made. Blacks have become the main characters of a number of shows, and they and other minorities routinely appear on others. Some TV mothers stay home—but some juggle full-time jobs with family life.

Some of this progress has been due to the efforts of **advocacy groups,** groups that exert pressure on the networks to correct stereotypes, to include more "real" characters and problems in the shows, and to hire more women and minorities behind the scenes. For example, the National Organization of Women organized studies of how women were being portrayed on television and used these studies to educate the networks. An Italian advocacy group, by organizing a boycott against sponsors of *The Untouchables,* got the producers to deemphasize Italian gangsters and add more good Italians to the series.

By the mid-1980s the networks were generally aiming for balance—negative portraits of groups balanced by positive ones, the pro side of a controversial issue balanced by the con side. **Standards and practices** committees at the networks now review scripts and invite comment from members of advocacy groups.

**Murder and mayhem.** According to some studies, by age sixteen, the average American has seen 200,000 acts of violence on television, including 33,000 murders. Each evening, the Big Three networks air about eight violent incidents an hour; children's cartoons average twenty-two per hour.

Does that matter? Some researchers believe it does. In a number of studies, groups of children or adults exposed to violent and nonviolent shows were then observed or surveyed about attitudes. Among those exposed to violent shows, there was a greater use of or tolerance for aggressive behavior in real life. This is how one researcher summarized a major study authorized by the Surgeon General: "We have impressive evidence that watching television violence causes a significant increase in aggressive behavior. It is not the only or even the most significant cause of antisocial behavior, but it certainly is one of the major contributors. It also happens to be one cause we *can* change."

Since violence does not appear to affect program ratings, the networks have shown little interest in reducing it or exploring alternatives. Critics, however, continued to pressure Congress and the networks. A bill passed in 1990 required the industry to adopt voluntary guidelines for curbing violent programming. Efforts by other lobbying groups, notably ACT (Action for Children's Television), have led to promises, at least, to deliver higher quality children's programming.

**Activity 5**

1. In pairs, analyze a group of people as they are presented in TV fiction: men, women, children, teenagers, blacks, other minorities, traditional families, nontraditional families, single people, elderly people. You will probably be able to come up with many ideas from memory, but try to watch relevant shows for specific examples.

2. Do the adults in your family monitor the shows you watch? Those watched by younger children in the family? Are there any shows you choose not to watch because they are controversial, offensive, or violent?

3. One novel suggestion for reducing violence on TV is to require shows to film it more realistically, complete with blood and gore. The theory is that viewers will be so disgusted they will demand an end. What do you think of this suggestion?

4. List the fiction shows you routinely watch. Label each with as many of the following as apply: Bland Escape, Realism Revealed, Stereotypes in Action, Balanced Ethnic View, Controversy Not OK, Violence Unleashed, Violence Tamed. Compare your responses with those of your classmates.

# Television as Information Source

News is the most obvious kind of nonfiction that television produces. And though TV is much more limited in its coverage than newspapers, it is the prime source of news for most Americans. Conciseness and visual appeal are its strengths. Writers and editors aim to convey as much information as possible in few words; often the visual tells part of the story.

Those visuals can be powerful indeed. During the Vietnam era the carnage of war was brought into the nation's living rooms and helped fuel the anti-war movement. Millions felt their feelings turn from excited joy to numb horror as the *Challenger* space shuttle exploded several seconds after lift-off in 1986, killing the crew of seven, including the first teacher-astronaut Christa McAuliffe.

The nation turns to television in times of celebration and of sorrow. The excitement and dignity of a presidential inauguration, the pageantry of a royal wedding, the "birthday bash" for the Statue of Liberty—television captures them and lets the nation celebrate, too. The funeral of a president, the devastation wrought by a hurricane, the horror of a plane crash—television captures these, too, and allows a nation to mourn.

Television has the power to unite the world. One-fifth of the population of the entire globe, 720 million people, watched in 1969 as Neil Armstrong emerged from his spacecraft and walked on the moon: "That's one small step for man, one giant leap for mankind." In 1985, thirteen satellites beamed the Live Aid concert to viewers in 150 countries, an event which raised $160 million of relief for starving African children.

Another nonfiction form, "video magazines," also ranks high with viewers. Network news magazines like *60 Minutes* and *20/20* allow television a forum for investigative journalism. In recent years local stations have developed their own video magazines in which they report on local items of interest—a craftsman who makes silver jewelry, a lighthouse that's now a private home, a museum that's worth a side trip.

The number of network **documentaries**—nonfiction reports—has declined, but the form is alive and well on public television and a number of cable channels. In addition to regular series like *Nova*, PBS produces specials like the 1990 eleven-hour report, *The Civil War*, which attracted an audience of

14 million, wowing critics and viewers alike. And cable channels like A&E and The Discovery Channel have opened a niche for independent filmmakers to report on everything from arctic wolves to festivals in Bali to the history of spices.

Documentaries are, of course, educational, but some PBS and cable programs also provide direct instruction. Televised classes can help you learn to speak Spanish, improve your SAT scores, or find out how to make cheese blintzes.

A new nonfiction form developed in the late 1980s is based on dramatizations of real events. Programs like *America's Most Wanted* and *Rescue 911* use a combination of real tapes, both audio and video, and "re-creations" to bring viewers the stories of true-life crimes and other dramatic events.

## Activity 6

1. What television nonfiction do you watch regularly? Why?

2. Are you ever assigned to watch certain shows as part of your work in English, science, or history class? Do your teachers use tapes as part of the curriculum? Do these help you to understand the subject? Why or why not?

3. What is the most recent celebration or sorrow, local or national, that dominated television? What advantages did the television cameras provide? Were there elements that you would criticize?

## Contestants and Talkers, Singers and Dancers

A healthy percentage of both critics and viewers alike believe that sports coverage is the best thing on TV—and certainly one of its major drawing cards. For live action, vivid pageantry, and compelling drama, sports presentations can't be beat. Video coverage of "the thrill of victory and the agony of defeat"—the phrase was popularized by ABC's *Wide World of Sports*—led to a number of technical and artistic improvements, too. Slow motion, freeze frame, stop action, and instant replay—techniques taken for granted today—owe their introduction to televised sports.

Sports are not the only games on television. Quiz and panel shows are immensely popular. Some have even spun off into board games that fans can play at home. Because game shows are inexpensive to produce, a flock of new ones have appeared on cable, some featuring children and teenagers as contestants.

Talk, both serious and trivial, is a staple on television. Late night talk shows, introduced in the 1950s, changed American sleeping habits. Sunday mornings see public affairs discussions, both local and national. Weekdays feature general talk shows like *Good Morning, America* and host-sponsored interviews like *Oprah Winfrey*.

Musical and variety shows were a lot more common in the early days of television. Today most network productions of such shows are specials featuring famous performers. PBS and the cable channel A&E televise concerts and musical dramas, but purists are not happy with the audio quality of these performances. In the future, advances in both audio and video quality are expected to revolutionize television's involvement with music.

All-music cable channels like MTV and TNN (The Nashville Network) are a matter of some controversy. Young people generally love them, and video experts praise their style and innovation, but critics claim they succeed only in luring young people away from more productive activities.

Comedy series like *Laugh In* are still aired as reruns, and newer comics have found audiences on a number of cable channels, often in the late-night hours.

**Activity 7**

1. Compare the experience of watching a sports event on TV and attending in person. Which do you prefer? Some critics worry that the volume of sports telecasting has led to reduced participation in sports. Is this true of you? Of adults you know?

2. Use a TV viewing guide to identify the current talk shows aired in the morning, afternoon, and late-night hours. Discuss the similarities and differences among the shows. Are you a fan of any of them? Why?

3. Do you like the music channels? Why or why not? What are some of the arguments you have heard against them? How would you respond?

## Children's Television

**Kidvid**, a term the industry uses for children's programming, is generally considered atrocious. One critic called it "a national embarrassment—a brain-rotting assault of animated comic books and shrieking commercials that border on child abuse." As well as being mindless and violent, many offerings are also exploitive—shows like *The Adventures of the Gummi Bears* and *Teenage Mutant Ninja Turtles,* which are essentially program-length commercials for candy or toys.

There are exceptions. Most PBS programs, like *Sesame Street* and *The Electric Company,* set the standard for quality children's programming. The cable station Nickelodeon has captured big audiences with kid versions of adult shows—a children's talk show, courtroom forums, game shows. Even the networks have managed occasional high-quality animated or storytelling shows. Shows like *Tiny Toon Adventures,* introduced in 1990, combined the fun of cartoons with thoroughly modern satire and lessons. Fox snagged adults as well as kids with its prime time animated show *The Simpsons*—and started the Big Three thinking about their own versions.

Nevertheless, in 1990 Congress passed major legislation requiring TV stations to improve the quality of children's programming. Yet the question remains: Who will judge that quality?

## Activity 8

Make a chart of the children's shows being offered by ABC, NBC, CBS, PBS, Fox, and Nickelodeon. As a class, rate each show as excellent, fair, or poor. (Skip any that class members are not familiar with.) Then rate each network.

## Talking It Over

**Some critics say the habits television fosters are its most potent force. Consider your own TV habits: How much TV do you watch? Do you watch specific shows—or do you watch television? (To answer this questions, consider two more: Do you have the set on even when you're doing other things? And if "your" show isn't on when you sit down, do you turn off the set or tune in to another channel?) Do you refuse opportunities for other activities because of shows you just can't miss? If you have a couple hours to fill, do you choose TV or some other activity? Do you videotape shows you otherwise couldn't watch so you can watch them later? Do you discuss shows with friends and relatives? Do you even think about them after they're over? After you have thought about these questions, decide which of the following statements reflects your judgment. Discuss your answers and opinions with your classmates.**

■ TV is creating a nation of "vidiots," who are addicted to the medium. They need a daily fix even if what they watch gives them no particular pleasure. They are consuming time that could be spent more profitably on other activities, and they are missing out on real life.

■ TV relieves the boredom that's a natural part of real life. Sometimes it provides high quality entertainment, and at worst allows a harmless way to relax. TV also gives viewers shared experiences, and food for thought and conversation.

## Advertisers and Ratings

The income of network television depends entirely upon advertising. The networks pay outside producers for programs and pay sports teams for the right to broadcast events. Then they sell spots to advertisers, with the cost based on the time slot, viewer demographics, and ratings. (Demographics, you remember, is the composition of the audience.) In 1988, for example, families watched *The Cosby Show,* women watched *Knots Landing,* men watched *L.A. Law,* and teenagers watched *The Wonder Years.* Advertisers made their choices according to the viewer they hoped to reach.

The most important ratings are determined by the **A.C. Nielsen Company.** A rating is the percentage of the population that watched a particular show. Nielsen gathers these figures through recording devices installed on the television sets of about 1,500 households around the country. Via telephone wires, these devices transmit signals to Nielsen offices about when the set is on and what channel it is tuned to. Two thousand other families maintain diaries for a week each month, noting who watched each show. You might think that the reports are based on an extremely small number of people, but the rating services use sophisticated sampling methods to choose households that in miniature reflect the population as a whole.

If you have ever cheered when your favorite show came back the next season or complained because it was cancelled, you already know something about the power of ratings. Since every rating point represents about 900,000 homes, you can see why even a small dip makes a big difference to advertisers. No matter how good a show is, or how loyal its viewers, if it doesn't have the ratings, it gets cancelled. Period. (Only one show, *Cagney & Lacey,* in the 1980s, ever returned after cancellation because of viewer pressure.)

In return for broadcasting the network's package of shows and commercials, local affiliates receive a portion of the advertising dollars and the right to sell a couple minutes per hour themselves. Nonaffiliated stations must sell all their advertising time themselves. Cable channels make money from both advertising and a portion of the fees viewers pay. Premium channels rely on the special viewer fees. PBS is funded by Congress, by grants from corporations and foundations, and by individual donations.

**A**ctivity **9**

1. Delegate a committee to find out the cost of a thirty-second spot commercial on a few of the class's favorite programs. Your public library may have a copy of the book *Standard Rate and Data,* or you can call the advertising department of the local station.

2. Of the three methods of funding television—through advertising, through user fees, and through tax and grant support—which do you prefer? What do you think of the suggestion that all TV become "pay per view"—that is, a fee for each show watched?

3. Poll the class to find out which shows it considers the worst on TV. What is so bad about them? For programs that have been on at least a year, discuss why they have survived.

## Summary

Television is undeniably one of the most potent forces in modern life. The sheer quantity of viewing—expanded by advances in cable and videotape recording—makes it a dominant activity in many people's lives. The Big Three networks—

NBC, CBS, and ABC—still dominate programming, but Fox, PBS, and a number of cable channels are challenging that position. TV fiction arguably makes this medium the storyteller of the nation, but critics worry about the message of its stories. Some say TV is at its best in nonfiction programs—news, sports, documentaries, direct instruction. While PBS is supported through government funding and grants, and cable through fees, commercial TV is entirely funded by advertising. Advertisers demand viewers, and so ratings become the key factor in what viewers get to see.

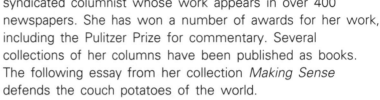

# **V**IEWPOINT

**E**llen **G**oodman is an associate editor for *The Boston Globe* and a syndicated columnist whose work appears in over 400 newspapers. She has won a number of awards for her work, including the Pulitzer Prize for commentary. Several collections of her columns have been published as books. The following essay from her collection *Making Sense* defends the couch potatoes of the world.

# **T**he Rise of the Couch Potato
## Ellen Goodman

One of the great pleasures in life is watching a lowly, disparaged and oppressed group of Americans come into their own. I am speaking of those maligned people known as couch potatoes. Or if you prefer, sofa spuds.

For the past decade, Jane Fonda, Richard Simmons and the entire medical establishment have led the rest of us down the aerobic path of life. We have spent our weekends and paychecks on leotards and lessons. We have bought bicycles to nowhere and suits to sweat in. Neither rain nor snow nor sleet has stopped us from speed walking.

But all this time, there existed among us a large number of low-profile Americans who showed true grit, strength of character and staying power. They sat out the jogging craze. They sat out the aerobic craze. High impact *and* low impact. They sat out racquetball. Indeed, they sat and sat.

While all around them, people were on the move, they remained rooted in front of the tube, exercising only their eyeballs. For this consistency, for their ability to not march to the beat of a distant drummer, they were vilified.

Couch potato was not a term of endearment. Indeed, many of us looked down upon these people, and not just because they were sitting. But all that is in the past. The couch-potato movement (if that isn't a contradiction of terms) is showing its newfound pride. The sofa spuds are flexing their muscles. Such as they are.

The year 1987 has become the year of the couch potato. They have at last risen up—without getting up, of course. They have begun to boast of the advantages, the life-style, of the easy chair.

After all, not one couch potato has ever come down with tennis elbow. Not one has ever had a shin splint. Maybe one or two got stiff fingers from pressing the TV remote, but they haven't suffered a single major injury. Except, of course, to their pride.

*New York* magazine, the herald of trends, was the first of the mainstream to put forth a cover story on couch potatoing as a new in-group activity this fall. We have now seen the growth of Potato Power. The Christmas marketplace boasts couch-potato dolls, a couch-potato quilt, couch-potato T-shirts.

I even received a trademarked Couch Potato Game: "the outrageous game that's played while you are watching TV." And I am told of a newsletter for those who network entitled "The Tuber's Voice."

In January, a couch-potato convention will be held in Chicago. It features, or so I read, a soap-opera seminar, a TV buffet dinner and a TV star lookalike.

Is it possible that we may live to see an Olympic event in marathon television watching? Or is this too American an event to go international? A founding father, Robert Armstrong, explains the potato philosophy this way: "We feel that watching TV is an indigenous American form of meditation." He calls it Transcendental Vegetation.

All this notoriety is wonderful news for those who spent years feeling down on themselves, not to mention their sofas. At last, they are getting their due.

But quite frankly, I have begun to worry. Will success spoil the spuds? Will all this attention—indeed, all this activity—encourage the great American couch potatoes to leave their posts and go out into the marketplace?

There is danger in the merchandising and exploitation of inaction. Will they ruin everything by developing some get-up-and go? Can a true member of the species play a board game and attend a convention without losing contact with his roots?

To find out the future of the couch potato, stay tuned to this station. And don't move a muscle. ■

## ☞ Your Turn

1. Write a humorous short story about a couch potato.
2. Write a humorous essay defending "vidiots," as Goodman does with couch potatoes.

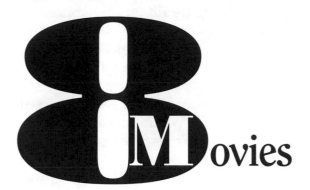

# 8 Movies

## The Role of Movies

The rustling hush as the theater lights dim and the screen lights up. The gradual loss of self as one is pulled into a different world. The sighs of the audience as the young lovers share their first kiss, the gasps as the murdered victim is revealed, the screams as the train hurtles out of the screen, the giggles as the fat elf begins yet another complaint.

**Vicarious experience,** that's what draws viewers to the movies—second-hand sensations that by the magic of film seem real for those short hours spent in the theater. The big screen and powerful audio create an almost hypnotic spell. And there's a communal element as well. You may have noticed that you react physically in a theater—your body becomes tense, you laugh out loud, you really shudder. These reactions spring from the chemistry between people in a large group watching the same movie. Watching television, even watching a videocassette of a movie on TV, is just not the same.

There is no question that the arrival of TV and later of cable movie channels and rental videos reduced the number of people going out to theaters. But the movie industry is still big business—it takes in about $5 billion a year on ticket sales, plus later sales to TV and video outlets.

Like book publishing, the movie industry derives little income from advertising. (Advertising in movies is not totally nonexistent, however. When you see an identifiable product brand on the screen—a soft drink, an airline, a cereal—the advertiser has paid for that plug.) But because the bulk of its income comes from the box office, a movie company must make movies that viewers are willing to pay to see; otherwise it will soon be out of business.

The drive to create art and the drive to make money have created tension within the movie industry between the serious film—a good movie, comic or dramatic, with a compelling message told with technical artistry—and the money-maker that aims only for your wallet. When actor Kevin Costner turned director with *Dances with Wolves* in 1990, he said he wanted to make a movie "that can make your face tingle. Movies should be about things that you'll never ever forget in your lifetime." Consumers—viewers like you—will decide if that is the kind of movie that will dominate in the future.

**Activity 1**

1. How do you decide which movies to see in a theater? To rent for home viewing? To watch on TV? Where do you get information about movies—from other people? From ads? From movie guides? From the box in the video rental store? How many movies would you say you watch a month? How does that compare with the number of books you read? How does it compare to the hours of non-movie TV you watch?

2. Many people equate movie greatness with the film's profitability. Check an almanac or other source to discover the all-time top-grossing movies and top video rentals. Of those you've seen, which would you call great movies? How do you account for the popularity of the movies on these lists?

## Finding a Vehicle

Like a book, a movie starts with an idea that becomes the basis for a manuscript—called a **screenplay.** Quite a lot of screenplays are based upon books—*Gone With the Wind, Scrooged, Jaws,* all started as novels. Others are based on stories originally written for the stage, like *The Sound of Music* and *Driving Miss Daisy.*

Books or plays that become best sellers or win awards are almost always **optioned**—a movie company pays the author a percentage for the right to produce the movie within a certain period of time, usually six to eighteen months. Filmmakers are eager to gain these rights because they know the stories have a built-in audience. By one producer's estimate, however, only one or two out of every 500 books optioned ever makes it to the screen.

Most screenplays are originals, written just for the screen. Beginners stand almost no chance of having their scripts read unless they can find an important agent willing to take them on. Agents in turn sell the screenplays to the studios. Or, the idea for a movie may originate with a producer, a director, or a star, and then a screenwriter will be hired to prepare the script. Some directors and stars write their own scripts; Woody Allen is a notable example.

Success spawns imitators, of course. *Rocky* was followed by *Rocky II, Rocky III, Rocky IV,* and *Rocky V,* and the 1980s saw a whole flock of movies related to the Vietnam War: *Platoon; Good Morning, Vietnam; Born on the Fourth of July;* and more.

**Activity 2**

1. Has reading a book ever inspired you to see the movie, or vice versa? For each example, which did you prefer? Why? What aspects of the book did the movie handle well? What were the differences between the two versions? Have you ever read a novelization of a movie? (A **novelization** is based on a screenplay but written in novel form. Many readers find them disappointing, but they are another way the movie company can make money.)

2. Of books you have read recently, which do you believe would make good movies? Write a short paper explaining why.

3. Some critics bemoan Hollywood's emphasis on the happy ending. Rocky Balboa was supposed to die at the end of *Rocky V,* but the filmmaker decided viewers wouldn't like that. What do you think? Of the last ten movies you have seen, how many have had happy endings? Sad endings? Open endings? (An open ending leaves some problems unresolved. Viewers must judge for themselves what happens next.)

## The People Who Make Movies

In the early days of movies, directors had little control. They were more like managers who saw to it that the studio's orders were carried out. Now, however, top directors are often as well known as the stars, and an ad may tout a movie as the new Steven Spielberg or Robert Altman film. Directors today oversee every aspect of the film, from script approval, shooting schedules, and camera angles to editing the final version of the film.

Directors still work with a studio, of course, and the big studios   Warner Brothers, Universal, Walt Disney—still finance big-budget pictures like *Batman* and *Who Framed Roger Rabbit.* But smaller, independent studios, sometimes started by directors or stars, also do important work. Sometimes these independent studios, like Ron Howard's Imagine Entertainment *(Parenthood),* affiliate with larger studios to take advantage of the big company's advertising and distribution muscle. Others, like New Line Cinema, go it alone and end up with hits like *Teenage Mutant Ninja Turtles.*

The producer of a movie, who was often the studio owner, used to have complete control. Nowadays the producer is usually in charge of such matters as finances, contracts, arranging for **locations** (real places where scenes will be shot), and advertising. Some directors also produce their own films.

The technical crew includes camera operators, film editors, electricians, costumers, makeup artists, set designers, animal handlers, and more—all the people you see listed in the credits at the end of a film. The cast includes the stars, the union performers who play the minor roles, and extras—professionals and nonprofessionals who are hired for nonspeaking roles or crowd scenes.

Performing in a movie is very different from performing on a stage. For a play, actors get into their roles and tell the audience a coherent story, beginning to end. They show anger, sympathy, fear, or humor in response to the ongoing action. Movie actors, by contrast, must perform according to the script, not what is going on around them. The fire raging in the street may be a special effect created in miniature on a studio table. But the actors supposedly watching the fire out an apartment window will have to show horror even though what they see is a perfectly ordinary street.

**A**ctivity **3**

Who are your favorite stars? Why do you like them—because of the movies they appear in? Because of their performances? For some other reason?

## Making a Movie

For filming, the movie is broken down into **shots** (specific camera actions), **scenes** (single shots or groups of shots that make up a discrete action), and **sequences** (coherent story segments—what viewers call a scene). Here for example, are two scenes from a sequence in which the two main characters meet each other on the street:

**86 MEDIUM SHOT**—Claudia is standing on sidewalk, oblivious of passersby. She glances at her watch and down the street.

*Cut to*

**87 LONG SHOT**—Claudia's view down the street, pedestrians approaching, Jack among them.

*Cut to*

**MEDIUM SHOT**—Jack, breaking into smile when he sees Claudia. Scene 86 includes just one shot, and Scene 87 includes two. Both take only a few seconds of the meeting sequence.

A **take** is a filming of a scene. If Jack stumbles in Scene 87, for example, the director will call for another take: "Take 2." Or the director may want to experiment with a different camera angle: "Take 3."

The director is guided by a shooting schedule that has nothing to do with the story's order of events. If a story goes back and forth between New York and the hills of Georgia, all the New York scenes will be filmed together and all the Georgia scenes together. Interior scenes may not be filmed at either location but in a set or building in Hollywood, Toronto, or London. (Actually, even the exterior scenes may not be shot where the story is set. It's fun to watch the credits and notice, for example, that the charming Maine fishing village is really in Washington state!) And some scenes—like an airplane taking off or a panorama of a city—may not be newly filmed at all, but **stock shots** from a film library.

Shooting on location takes a great deal of preparation. What with arranging for the area to be closed to traffic, obtaining permission to film various buildings, planning costumes and **props** (properties—physical objects needed for a scene), transporting the cast and crew, setting up the cameras, and more, a scene of just a few minutes running time may take days to film.

How about sound? Some sound is recorded live, of course, but much is dubbed in afterwards. Special effects and disaster sounds—even ordinary sounds like a high wind or a door closing—can be added from recorded collections. You can't even be sure of the voices. Audrey Hepburn starred in *My Fair Lady*, but another singer's voice was dubbed in for her songs.

Once the movie is shot, it goes to the cutting room, where the important work of editing is done. The director works closely with the editor, choosing from among the miles of film what pieces will be used and where. Each scene and take was marked during filming so particular segments can be found easily.

The advertising department now begins hyping the film on TV and in trade magazines. Movie companies invest huge sums to promote their films. Even an independent may spend a million dollars to advertise a film that cost $2 million to make. A major studio with a potential blockbuster may spend $20 million in advertising.

Copies of the final film go to distributors and from them to theaters who rent the film for a period of time. Theaters also receive promotional materials—posters for the lobby and ads they can run in the local media.

**Activity 4**

1. What movies are currently being advertised on TV? What claim does each make? What images does it feature? Have you ever been disappointed in a movie you went to see because you were attracted by its ad?

2. Observe the movie posters at a local theater and scan the movie ads in your local paper. Now create a poster or ad for a movie you've seen recently.

# Behind the Camera

If you have ever looked at a strip of film, you know that a movie isn't really a "moving picture" at all but a series of still shots presented so fast—twenty-four frames per second—that the eye sees them as moving. For animated films, artists break down movement into very small changes, each of which is drawn and photographed, and then shown at twenty-four frames per second. One director estimated that a competent animator could produce about six seconds of film a week. You might be interested to know the *cels*—individual celluloid frames—from famous animated films are collectors' items. Would you pay six figures for a hand-painted image of Donald Duck?

Both animated and regular movies are an incredibly skillful blend of carefully planned and edited camera shots. Filmmakers know how various shots work in viewers, minds and manipulate those shots to create the desired effect. Here are some of the techniques they use to bring you a movie:

**Focus.** How much you see in a particular scene depends on how the camera lens is focused. A **long shot** shows the whole scene—perhaps the main character and the room where she's standing. A **medium shot** comes in closer—the character standing by the window. A **close-up** moves in further—to the character's hands fiddling restlessly with a ring. An **extreme close-up** focuses on a detail—the ring itself.

Long, medium, and close-up shots are often used in that order because that's how the mind works when presented with a new scene. You walk into a room, get a general impression, focus on the person who greets you, and then notice the shirt he's wearing. The reverse order can create surprise—a close-up of a peaceful face, a medium shot of a man lying on the grass, a long shot that reveals it's a corpse in the park. The camera can also **zoom** in or out, changing focus quickly from wide angle to close-up or vice versa.

At the beginning or end of a sequence, the director can allow the camera focus to **fade in** to a sharp, clear picture or **fade out** to misty brightness or complete darkness. Or the camera can focus clearly on part of the subject and leave the rest of the scene slightly out of focus.

**Filters.** Filters on the camera lens can change the color or mood of a scene, making a drab scene look bright or vice versa. Many of the exterior scenes of *Batman* were shot through a red filter to give an eerie glow to the city, and *Fiddler on the Roof* was shot with a nylon stocking over the lens to give the film a warm, earthy, slightly hazy feeling.

**Angle.** When the camera is at eye level, you get a "normal" view of the subject. But a "low-angle shot," with the camera looking up at the subject, makes the subject look bigger and more imposing. A **high-angle shot,** with the camera looking down at the subject, makes it look small, weak, or lonely. The monster in a horror movie, seen from below, becomes even more terrifying. The monster's victim, seen from above, looks helpless.

**Movement.** Movement can be recorded by a hand-held camera, but is more often controlled with other equipment. With the camera on a tripod, the operator can **pan** by swiveling the camera from side to side or **tilt** by swiveling it up and down. Mounted on a wheeled **dolly,** the camera can move smoothly toward or away from the subject. The camera can **track** a moving subject when it is mounted on another moving object—in a second car tracking the subject car, for example. A scene can be filmed in **slo-mo** (slow motion) to intensify a moment.

**Cuts.** In film language, to cut means to change the shot. When the director yells, "Cut!" that ends a particular shot, either because a mistake has been made or because that segment is complete. Later, in the editing room, that spot may be literally cut and the segment spliced to whatever comes next.

A **cut-in** focuses viewer attention on a specific subject. The camera may pan the crowd in a courtroom, for example, and then suddenly cut in to a shot of the defendant. A **cut-away** shifts the camera from one action to another.

One scene may show two people talking in a room, and the next will cut away to the detective listening outside the window.

Viewers accustomed to the conventions of movies and videos accept the use of cut-aways to shrink distance and time. A girl steps into a bus and the bus moves away from the camera. A fraction of a second later the camera picks up the girl's mother at home. Or the camera records the chatter of some people on a plane, cuts away to an exterior shot of the plane, cuts again to the plane touching down, and finally comes back to the couple, now emerging into the terminal. Viewers accept the "magic" of shifting locations and compressing time.

**Activity 5**

1. Many of the techniques you have just read about are also used by still photographers. In newspapers and magazines, find examples of photographs that represent a long shot, a medium shot, a close-up, an extreme close-up, an unusual focus, a probable use of filters, a low-angle shot, and a high-angle shot. Label the examples and include them in your media log.

2. Spend a class period watching part of a movie video and identify the various shots. Have someone control the video so the class can pause for discussion or go back to something it missed.

## Kinds of Movies

Movies can be classified in genres, just like books and television shows. You are probably already familiar with most of them—musicals, dramas, comedies, westerns, romances, thrillers, action pictures, war movies, disaster movies, horror movies, children's movies, animated films. In recent years, many studios have produced teen movies with teenage protagonists specifically targeted to teenage viewers—movies like *Dirty Dancing, The Karate Kid,* and *The Breakfast Club.* These are often released during the summer to draw kids with time to fill and money from summer jobs.

By agreement with the Motion Picture Association of America, movies carry a label as a guide to viewers: **G** (suitable for general audiences); **PG** (parental guidance suggested); **PG-13** (parental guidance suggested for children under 13); **R** (restricted; children under 17 not admitted unless accompanied by an adult); **NC-17** (no children under 17 admitted).

You can find both good and bad movies among every category of film. Movie reviewers on TV and radio and in magazines and newspapers evaluate the quality of movies and make recommendations about who might like them— if anyone. Movie reviewing is a highly subjective business, however, so it isn't uncommon for different reviewers to disagree wildly about a particular film.

It is also not uncommon for a movie company to seize on the one good thing a reviewer has to say about a bad movie to use in an ad.

In terms of making money, the most important award a movie can win is the **Academy Award,** or **Oscar,** presented by the Academy of Motion Picture Arts and Sciences. Theoretically, these awards go to the best movies for various accomplishments—best picture, best actor, best musical score, best costume design, and so on—but a lot of politicking goes on. Movie companies will often release potential winners in the fall, before the December 24 deadline, so they'll be fresh in the minds of the judges. They also advertise these movies in the trade magazines and court Academy members at private screenings.

In the view of serious critics, the Oscars are a mixed bag. Sometimes they indeed go to excellent films, even to **sleepers**—movies that play better than expected—but sometimes influence seems more important than quality.

**A**ctivity **6**

1. As a class, make a list of current and recent movies targeted to children and teenagers. Which have you seen and liked? Why?

2. In an almanac or other source, find a list of recent Oscar winners. Which of these movies have you seen? Do you think the awards were deserved?

3. Make a list of five to ten movies you consider your all-time favorites. (Both reviewers and regular viewers enjoy doing this.) Be prepared to discuss why you like these movies.

4. Read a number of reviews of current movies. Choose one for a movie you might like to see and analyze the review. Does the reviewer recommend the movie? For general audiences or for a particular group? What criteria (standards) did the reviewer seem to use in judging the movie; that is, what aspects did he or she discuss—the story? the acting? the directing? the **cinematography** (camera work)? the total effect?

5. Now view a movie with the eyes of a critic. Using what you learned about reviewing in exercise 4, write a review.

## Talking It Over

Young people enjoy horror movies, but are these movies good for them? Some horror movies aim for artistry—but many are exploitive, reveling in blood, mayhem, and special effects. Some fans watch only "good" horror films, but others go for anything with a drooling monster or dripping knife in the ad. What do you think of this trend? Consider the horror movies you've seen and heard about. Then decide which statement below better reflects your judgment. Discuss your examples and reasons with your classmates.

■ I think most horror movies are sick. A steady diet of them desensitizes viewers to horror in real life. Adults and young viewers alike should stop supporting these movies, and parents should exercise more control over what their kids watch.

■ I think most horror movies are just good, creepy fun. Viewers are used to them, so it's not hard to separate fantasy from real life. Parents needn't monitor what their kids watch; kids are pretty good judges of what they can tolerate.

## Summary

Though television has challenged the movie industry, watching a movie is still a unique and absorbing media experience. The screenplay for a movie may be based on a book or play, but more often it is an original story. In filmmaking today, the director controls most of what you see, from selecting a script to filming and editing. The screenplay is written in shots, scenes, and sequences, and is filmed according to a practical schedule. Cinematography (camera work) is carefully planned. Focus, filters, movement, cuts—these techniques and more are an integral part of movie making. Advertising, reviews, and awards can contribute to the success of a movie, but ultimately viewers decide what movies they will support.

# VIEWPOINT

**Jeff MacNelly**, a winner of three Pulitzer Prizes, is a syndicated cartoonist who uses the characters in his strip to comment with humor and bite on contemporary life. The practice of taking a few positive words from an otherwise negative review and using these words to advertise a movie is not as common as it once was. Still, Jeff MacNelly reminds us that it is not a practice altogether unknown, and one that you should be alert to in dealing with movie ads.

# ☛ Your Turn

1. Find a negative review of a movie. Then create a newspaper ad for that movie that capitalizes on positive words used in the review. Highlight the parts of the review you used and present both the review and your ad on a poster.

2. Write a negative review of a movie you have seen recently but use only positive words to do so. In short, use exaggeration to mock the movie.

# 9 Radio and the Recording Industry

## The Theater of the Mind

**R**adio is now closer to the people than any other medium.

—William O'Shaughnessy

Radio used to fulfill the role television fills today. During the 1930s and 1940s, the Golden Age of Radio, families gathered around the radio just as they gravitate to TV now.

They listened as President Franklin Roosevelt addressed the nation in his fireside chats, raising their hopes during the Depression and inspiring their courage during the war years. They listened to newscasters whose words provided the visuals: "Berlin was a kind of orchestrated hell, a terrible symphony of light and flame," reported Edward R. Murrow after a bombing raid in World War II.

They listened to music, to the big band sounds of Tommy Dorsey and Benny Goodman, to crooners like Bing Crosby and jazz greats like Ella Fitzgerald. They listened to sports, sometimes with the play-by-play provided by sportscasters distant from the action, reading off teletype reports and accompanying their commentary with sound effects that reproduced the crack of the bat on the ball and the roar of the crowd. They tuned in to game shows and talk shows and the first soap operas—*Ma Perkins, Stella Dallas, Road of Life,* and other problem-packed dramas that went on for years.

On programs like *Lux Radio Theater* and *The First Nighter,* they heard movies rewritten for radio and plays written specially for this medium. They listened to comedy sketches and the forerunners of the sitcom—Edgar Bergen and Charlie McCarthy, Jack Benny, George Burns and Gracie Allen.

Children waited eagerly for *Little Orphan Annie, Dick Tracy, Superman, Captain Midnight,* and the *Lone Ranger.* The whole family shivered over the spooky stories on *Lights Out* and *I Love a Mystery.* "Who knows what evil lurks in the hearts of men?" intoned a heavy-voiced lead-in. "The Shadow knows."

Do not underestimate these radio dramas. Marvelous voices, exquisite pauses, and realistic sound effects kept listeners on the edge of their seats. Sound effects were "invented," in fact, to give that touch of realism to the stories. The NBC studio at one time had its own huge train bell, a locomotive whistle, and equipment that could re-create the click-click of the wheels and the whoosh of the steam pipe. With a few simple items—cellophane paper, rice running down a tube, a cookie sheet—sound experts could make listeners hear a fire, a storm, a roll of thunder. Their voices could provide a horse's whinny, a monkey's screech, a lion's roar. Eventually, radio dramas began to draw their effects from collections of recorded sounds, a technique that is still used in TV and movies today.

The power of radio drama was vividly revealed in 1938 when the CBS *Mercury Theater on the Air* broadcast Orson Welles' version of the H.G. Wells story *War of the Worlds*. So realistic were the "news bulletins" about the landing of the Martians, the "scientific commentary" by experts, the "panic" of fleeing Earthlings, that listeners all over the country became convinced an actual invasion was taking place. Police stations and newspapers were deluged with frantic calls. People rushed screaming into the street, or fell on their knees in prayer, or rushed home to protect their loved ones.

Though electronic storytelling is today the province of television, there are those who still mourn the lost days of radio drama. To listen to a drama on radio is a very different experience. Television does not demand creativity from the viewer; it presents a pre-packaged experience. Radio, by contrast, stimulates the imagination to fill in the visuals. Listeners see the drama in their heads. They set the scene, flesh out the characters, move the action— they are participants.

**A***ctivity* **1**

1. Borrow two or three recorded collections of old radio shows from your library or other source and listen to them as a class. How do the programs compare with TV shows today? How does the experience differ from that of TV?

2. Two people are chatting as they drive home. It starts to rain. They pull up, dash out of the car and into the house, slam the door—and hear something ominous. In small groups, write short scenes like this one and then prepare a tape that reveals the power of sound effects. Experiment with your voices, real action, and simple objects. Dialogue cues can help, too: "Was that thunder?" "Here, kitty!" or "Is it okay to burn this in the fireplace?" Play your tape for the class and discuss how the sound effects were created.

## Radio Today

Today radio is everywhere—in kitchens, bedrooms, and bathrooms, in cars and elevators, on the beach, and on the street. People tune in while they jog and while they do homework. They buy tiny pocket versions and huge boom boxes. They remain glued to battery-operated radios in emergencies when power outages silence the TV.

But what they hear is very different from the programs of the Golden Age. Today, music and talk dominate the air waves.

The major networks—CBS, NBC, and ABC—started as radio broadcasters. Though these networks still own and affiliate with radio stations, they now play almost no role in programming. Radio stations today specialize; they **format** their programming to snag a target audience—young people, home-makers, commuters, insomniacs. Most can be classified by their format: Top 40, R&B (rhythm and blues), C&W (country-western), easy listening, oldies, classical, all-news, religious, foreign language, or talk shows.

Most MOR (middle-of-the-road) stations offer a mix of news, talk, light popular music, traffic reports, and community service announcements. Some offer a consumer advocacy service that tries to solve callers' problems with government agencies or businesses. Some have advice programs during which listeners can call for help on relationships, gardening, or car care. Some feature a date-line on which individuals present taped information about themselves. Community radio stations, sometimes reaching only a few miles, broadcast school sports, local news and features, and a lost-and-found.

The Corporation for Public Broadcasting, the parent organization of PBS, also affiliates with local radio stations under the banner of National Public Radio (NPR). These stations usually offer a mixture of news, public affairs programs, and music—classical, jazz, electronic, folk, ethnic. They also offer radio dramas and readings from well-known books.

DJs (disc jockeys) and talk masters in some cities become "personalities" who command huge audiences. Top 40 stations sometimes hire a syndicated service, complete with DJ, or specially train their own to maintain a high level of excitement. Talk masters often organize their shows around a guest speaker— a politician, an author of a recent book, a colorful local person—and invite callers to respond with questions and comments. Some talk masters are famous for their manner—their liberal or conservative politics, their sharp-tongued wit, their willingness to tackle controversial topics.

At many radio stations, news is restricted to about five minutes on the hour. Because only essential information is given, radio news is sometimes called "headline news." Stations affiliated with a national network may use a segment from the network in addition to their local report. Community sta-tions often hire reporters to cover local news live or on tape; bigger stations prepare occasional interpretive or investigative series.

All-music stations can operate with very few employees since the entire day's broadcast can be programmed and handled by computer.

Like TV stations, radio stations operate on a license from the FCC. They broadcast on either the AM or FM band, their channel numbers corresponding to specific radio wave frequencies. An AM (amplitude modulation) station is assigned one of a possible 107 frequencies between 54 and 160 kilocycles (thousands of cycles per second), and an FM station one of a hundred channels between 88 and 108 megacycles (millions of cycles per second). AM signals can travel much farther than FM signals and even further at night though the range also depends on the power of the transmitter. FM signals, while limited in range, produce a superior sound, free of interference and static. Both AM and FM can broadcast in stereo, but not all radios are equipped to pick up AM stereo. By 1978 more listeners, including young people, were tuning in to FM than AM.

**Activity 2**

1. Count the number of radios in your household; don't forget car radios. Have one class member tally the results and work out the class average.

2. Divide the AM and FM bands among a number of small groups. Each group should scan its chunk, pausing at every signal to identify the station's *frequency, call letters, format,* and *target audience.* Chart the results in your media log.

3. Listen to half an hour of one station (each student a different station) and list all the products and services advertised. Check this list against the target audience you identified in exercise 2. Is there a relationship?

4. List and characterize the radio personalities you can name. Then ask a couple of adults you know to do the same. Compare the results.

5. Is your community served by a station that provides local news, sports, and other topics of local interest? Spend a class period listening to this station (or a taped segment, if the station broadcasts music during the class time) and discuss how well it serves the public interest.

6. Hold a discussion of the class's radio habits: What are your favorite stations? Why? Do you ever tune in to other stations for a particular purpose? Do you like some of the talk shows or other kinds of programs?

## The Recording Industry

Recorded music gained just as radio did, from advances in audio technology. If you've ever listened to old 78 records, you know how tinny they sound—yet they were regarded as miraculous when they first appeared. By contrast, today's compact disc (CD), played on good equipment, produces a sound that some audiophiles (those who love recorded music) claim is superior to a live performance.

For years, vinyl records (along with tapes, in later years) dominated the recording industry, but the 1980s witnessed an almost complete turnover to

CDs. Some stores no longer even stock records, though tapes have held their own. The enormous sales of blank tapes attest to listeners' interest in packaging their own favorites by recording off the radio or other people's collections. Music videos on laser discs and digital audio tape (DAT) are the newest recording media.

The Recording Industry of America, Inc., gives gold, platinum, and multi-platinum awards to top-selling recordings according to the following formula:

| **Award** | **Number Sold** | | |
| --- | --- | --- | --- |
| | *Singles* | *Albums* | *Music Videos* |
| Gold | 1 million | 500,000 | 25,000 |
| Platinum | 2 million | 1 million | 50,000 |
| Multi-Platinum | 3 million | 2 million | 100,000 |

Of recordings issued in 1988 and 1989, one single, eleven music videos, and twenty-three albums earned multi-platinum awards. By anybody's account, that's mass communication.

Figures like these and accounts in fan magazines about the extravagant lifestyles of top performers inspire a lot of young people to aim for the top themselves. As in book publishing, however, many try and few succeed—and even fewer make the fabulous money of the biggest stars.

But an aspiring musician faces a problem an aspiring author needn't worry about: it costs a great deal of money even to be heard by a recording company. Though a few of the smaller radio stations will play tapes by unknowns, the usual process is this: Say a group—call them Double Digit—has been getting rave reviews from the schools and small clubs where they've been playing. They have a song one of the members wrote (otherwise, they'll eventually have to pay royalties to whoever owns the song). Now they must rent a sound studio, with its engineers and equipment, create a master tape of their song, and make a demo (demonstration recording) from the tape. Double Digit foots the bill for all of this.

Now the group must find someone to listen to the demo, so copies go out to recording companies. As with book manuscripts, most demos are rejected, but let's say Double Digit gets a contract offer. That contract will guarantee the group a royalty—a percentage of each recording sold. Certain production and publicity expenses typically come out of the group's share, however.

So Double Digit records the song professionally and the record company works to get air time for it. How much effort the company devotes to promotion depends on how confident it feels about Double Digit's sound. If listeners take to the song and begin buying it, Double Digit may be on the way. More likely, the song will be a flop—and Double Digit will have to start over.

Even if the song is a modest success, Double Digit is not yet on Easy Street. By now they've hired a producer, a manager, an agent, an accountant, perhaps a lawyer—and all these people want to be paid, too. Double Digit gets a concert tour—but many of the expenses come out of the band members' pockets.

Thousands of people make a respectable living or at least extra income in music—in groups and in orchestras, as studio musicians and club performers—but the gold ring is not easy to grab. The gold ring is not the only joy of performing, however. As a medium of personal communication, it can be a lifetime source of pride, relaxation, and pleasure.

**Activity 3**

1. Estimate how much money you contribute to the music industry each year. About how many recordings do you buy a month? Multiply this by twelve and again by the average cost of a CD or tape. How many concerts do you attend? Add the ticket price to your figure. Do you buy spin-off products, like posters or T-shirts? If so, add the cost of these. Compared to other things you spend money on, how important are your music expenditures?

2. Check an almanac or music magazine to find out who the current top-selling performers are. How many are your favorites? How long have they been your favorites? Why does the popularity of most performers flare and die within just a few years?

3. Write a report on your favorite performer or group. Do research to discover how they got started and how well they are doing now. Also analyze their appeal: Why do you and others like them? What is distinctive about their songs or their sound?

# The Message of Popular Music

Popular music existed as far back as people made music, but it was the twentieth century that turned popular music into a form of mass communication. Before this century, listeners were limited by distance—they had to be close enough to the performers to hear their voices or instruments.

Most of today's popular music had its roots in jazz, an American musical form that arose from African drum rhythms, black spirituals, work songs, and old fiddlers' tunes. Dixieland, ragtime, blues, boogie-woogie, swing, hop, rock 'n' roll, rap—all derive from jazz. Rumba, mambo, cha-cha, reggae, salsa—jazz with a Latin beat.

The heart of jazz and its offspring is rhythm, with the beat falling differently than it does in art music. That rhythm *is* the message, whether listeners sit back and enjoy or jump up to dance.

Add lyrics and you find another message. The best of popular music, like good short stories or poems, can etch a powerful comment about life and the human condition. You can find countless examples of jazz, blues, rock, and rap songs that speak powerfully and realistically of the joy and pain of growing up, of love, of workday woes and political problems.

But as with other mass media, the recording industry has its critics who point to the sentimental, unrealistic picture of youth or love or happiness that many songs convey—a message that can give listeners distorted ideas. Other popular songs are vulgar, racist, sexist, materialistic, or hate-filled. What is the message of songs like these? To say the message has no effect is naive. At the very least, it reveals a culture that still has not solved some of its most serious problems.

**Activity 4**

1. Prepare a taped report on your favorite musical form— classical, jazz, rock, C&W. Define this form and identify its distinctive characteristics. Prove your points with musical examples.

2. Consider your favorite instrumental numbers. What is the message of the music? You may not find it easy to translate your experience into words, but try to examine both your physical and emotional response.

3. As a class, nominate current popular songs in three categories: worthy lyrics, sappy lyrics, and warped lyrics. Have class members write out the lyrics to a couple songs in each category and discuss their messages. Do you think sentimental and offensive lyrics have an effect on listeners?

4. **Grammy** awards are given each year to outstanding records and albums as judged by the National Academy of Recording Arts and Sciences. Check an almanac or other source to identify recent Grammy winners. Do you agree with the choices? If not, what recordings in recent years would you have honored?

5. Whether recordings with sexually explicit lyrics should be labeled is a controversial issue. Some say that the labels violate free-speech rights and only make the recordings more appealing to the young. Others say the labels help parents monitor their children's listening. Currently, such labels are voluntary. Do you think labels should be required by law? Why or why not?

# Talking It Over

The producer—often called the A&R (artist and repertory) man or woman—is a key figure in the production of many popular songs. Working in a control booth, this person creates the sound you hear in the recording, muting some sounds, enhancing others, building in an echo effect, "overdubbing" a voice (so one voice sounds like two or more), creating sounds electronically that no acoustic instrument could produce. After the recording session, the producer splices bits and pieces of tape together to create the finished master tape. The final sound in many cases is like nothing that could be done live—which is why some popular artists are disappointing in concert and why others must lip-sync on stage. Consider songs you know in which production techniques are especially important. Then decide which statement below better reflects your judgment. Discuss your examples and opinion with your classmates.

■ I think it's silly to be a fan of any performer or group whose recordings are really the result of production techniques. It's fine to like the songs, but a concert by this kind of performer or group is fake and a waste of money.

■ Music is music; the sound is what's important, not how it's produced. If you're a fan of a performer or group that's heavy on production techniques, you're really a fan of the total package, and I think that's perfectly legitimate.

## Summary

Radio used to offer much more varied fare than it does today; in fact, it used to be as varied as current television programming and really laid the ground-work for today's television shows. Radio stations must be licensed by the FCC, and while some are network-affiliated, the networks have little to do with programming. Most stations can be classified by their format, with middle-of-the-road and public stations having the most varied programming. Radio depends heavily on the recording industry, itself a mass medium. Making the big time in recording is no easier than in any other medium, but that fact should not dilute the pleasure of performing or listening. Recorded music and songs have a message; listeners should be attuned to what that message is.

**VIEWPOINT**

**Les Brown** has been a radio and television reporter, reviewer, and editor for a number of publications, including *Variety* (the weekly newspaper of the entertainment industry), *The New York Times*, and *Channels* magazine. He has also lectured on media at colleges and universities and has authored many books, including *Les Brown's Encyclopedia of Television*. In the following excerpt from *Electric Media*, Brown lovingly recalls the enchantment of radio before television inherited some of its functions.

# Radio, the Parent Reborn
## Les Brown

When the power blew all over the Northeast during the great blackout of 1965, the voices in the darkness that steadied millions of bewildered people came over transistor and car radios.

A group of us stranded at an old printing plant in the Bronx learned from a tiny receiver (which happily someone had had in his pocket) that we were not alone in our plight, and once informed of what had gone wrong we patiently waited it out, feeling safe ourselves but concerned with how the blackout was affecting others. We hovered over that little radio, the bunch of us, dependent on its steady dispatches as our only contact with the outside. Radio was a brilliant communicator that night, and undoubtedly because of it there was little hysteria among the affected and surprisingly few casualties of the power failure.

A medium much taken for granted and usually connected in our minds with recordings and chatter demonstrated an inherent superiority over the other media and probably saved hundreds of lives. The portability of radio, the compactness of it, the ease with which it can relay voices from distant points, the speed with which it can deliver news bulletins, its ready adaptability to emergencies, and finally its transcendence of plug-in electricity all came into play, as they had many times in heroic performances elsewhere in the country during calamities.

But commercial radio survives in America as only a faint echo of its old self, although nicely enough as a business. For those who were not alive before there was television, it is well to know what radio used to be, for its real powers are far from realized today. Some day the medium-that-was may be rediscovered. Reflecting on the time when *it* was that magic box in our homes, for twenty-five years before the end of World War II, I find it still anything but backward or primitive.

We spoke then of radio playing in the *theater of the mind.* Through sound and the suggestion of language, radio created images which we, sitting in our living rooms, felt we were seeing. Words could make us smell the cake baking in the oven, and scenery was painted in a phrase. Everything in the theater of the mind was in color and three dimensions.

There was a show every week called *The First Nighter,* which pretended the listener would be *seeing* a Broadway play on opening night at "the little theater off Times Square." As a child of ten or twelve in Chicago, I liked the program's opening more than any of its romantic little dramas. Amidst a beeping of horns and the stirring of a crowd, a car door opened and closed (I imagined a black limousine), and a voice was heard to say, "Good evening, Mr. First Nighter." (That would be me, in white tie and tails.) Then, over the growing crowd noises, a page called, "Curtain going up." And then, a lowering of sound, a shuffling silence, and the announcer saying in hushed tones, "The footlights are lit—and here's our show." I was transported into the adult elegance of Broadway a thousand miles from my home.

One day I learned that the show was not produced in New York at all but in my own city, Chicago, and when I was taken to see one of the performances at the studio, there were only a few actors at the microphone dropping their used pages of script carefully to the floor, an orchestra behind them, and a sound-effects man with his amazing apparatus off to the side. It was he who created New York and opening night for me every week. Disillusioned, I thought I would never enjoy the show again, but the next time it came on, all the magic was intact.

That wasn't even my favorite program, although I'm at a loss to say what was. I seemed to like everything—the soap operas, the mysteries, the musicales, *The Lone Ranger,* the glittering comedy hours with Jack Benny, Fred Allen, Bob Hope, Red Skelton, and Eddie Cantor, and even the fellow at the piano with the laughing voice who entertained the kiddies on Saturday morning. *Let's Pretend* was a knockout show, and so were *I Love a Mystery* and *Vic and Sade,* but as I grew older and the war went on I listened with awe to the incredibly graphic dispatches of Edward R. Murrow from the rooftops of London.

His reports, delivered against the actual sounds of war, were rich in imagery, so that you saw—and felt—as you listened to hard details. He lit up one of his reports with the ominous line:

"It's a bomber's moon tonight."

Recounting an air raid on Germany, to which he was an eyewitness from one of the planes, he told of incendiary bombs "going down like a fistful of rice on a piece of black velvet," and when it was over, he said:

"Berlin was a kind of orchestrated hell, a terrible symphony of light and flame."

Murrow's word pictures were usually in color. Describing a paratrooper operation from a plane, he spoke of the chutists looking like so many "khaki dolls hanging beneath a green lamp shade."

Sightless radio prodded the poet in Murrow. How brilliant a wordsmith he was, and, as I came later to know, how brilliant a journalist.

Television with its real picture inherited it all, Murrow included, and radio went through years of economic convulsions, scrambling to stay in business until it settled into the feasible recorded music and information patterns that characterize it today. ■

## ☛ Your Turn

1. The essay you have just read is a piece of **nostalgia**—a warm, fond look at the past. Choose something from your own past you remember fondly (it need not be related to media; you could choose, for example, a favorite toy, a place you lived, a childhood game). Then write a nostalgic essay recapturing its magic.

2. Fewer than fifty years separate the radio of Les Brown from the radio you know. Forecast what radio will be like fifty years in the future. Then write a humorous essay describing it *or* a nostalgic retrospective of radio today.

# 10

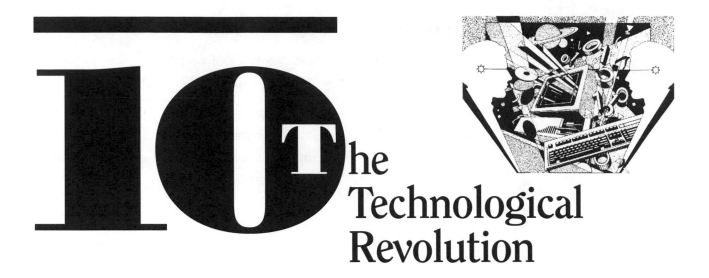

# The Technological Revolution

## The Role of Technology

The history of mass media parallels the history of the technology that makes it possible. As you have seen, print media—books, newspapers, and magazines—owe their existence to the invention of movable type in the fifteenth century. The invention of the telegraph and the telephone in the nineteenth century and of the wireless telegraph in the early twentieth century paved the way for radio, television, and the recording industry. Advances in photography in the nineteenth century, along with the turn-of-the-century idea to project a number of sequenced photographs, led to movies.

The late-nineteenth and twentieth centuries witnessed explosive advances in the equipment used to produce media messages. In 1877, for example, Thomas Edison demonstrated that a stylus tracing indentations in a cylinder covered with tinfoil produced an audible sound. That beginning led to the Victrola (a trade name for the first phonograph), the electronic phonograph, hi-fi (high-fidelity phonographs), stereo, and the laser disk player. Steps along the way were made possible by improvements in microphones, amplifiers, speakers, plastics, magnetic tape, and laser light.

The introduction of the computer in the mid-1900s also had enormous impact on mass media. As you have seen, computers connected to audio equipment can be programmed to broadcast an entire day's radio fare, music and advertising, reducing the staff necessary to run a radio station to two— an engineer on stand-by in case something goes wrong and an announcer to give hourly news updates. Computer-controlled satellites bring the whole world to your living room. You can watch a live discussion between high officials halfway around the globe from each other. You can be a spectator of Olympic games held in Korea, Canada, France—anywhere. Computer-controlled cameras on spaceships bring you photographs of Mars, Venus, and Jupiter.

There is no question that this explosion has affected personal life and human culture. If you had been born anytime before the twentieth century, chances are good you would have spent your life eking out existence on a farm, seldom, if ever, traveling more than five miles from your home. Only occasionally would you have received word of what was happening beyond your village. Today, even if you live on a farm, you are surrounded by books, magazines, newspapers, radios, television, and movies that make you a citizen of the world.

"And you ain't seen nothin' yet."

**Activity 1**

1. Using the figures you came up with in various chapters, update the chart you prepared for Activity 1 in Chapter 1. Work out the average number of hours per day you are involved with media. Subtract the average number of hours you sleep from twenty-four, divide that number into your media hours and multiply by 100. The result is the percentage of your waking life you spend with media.

2. Your teacher will divide the class into small groups, each assigned a medium: print (books, magazines, and newspapers), radio, television, movies, the recording industry, and computers. Your group should research and prepare an oral report on the technological development of this medium—the equipment that made it possible. Include an illustrated chart that highlights important dates and developments.

## Technology and Print Media

Until the invention of the computer, advances in print technology meant improvements in quality rather than outright changes—with one exception. That was the invention of the telegraph in the mid-nineteenth century, which let reporters wire their stories home and got information to people much quicker than before.

But the arrival of the computer absolutely revolutionized the print industry. Gone are the days when reporters pecked out their stories on manual typewriters, rushed the typed sheets to their editors for comments, and rushed back to retype. Now in most large newspaper offices, reporters work on word processors, and editors have only to tap buttons on their own keyboards to call up the stories. Gone are the copy boys and copy girls who ran the stories to the typesetters—and in many print facilities, gone are the typesetters. Now editors send stories to the composing room via the computer, and the computer prepares the master from which the printing is done.

Typed manuscripts still arrive by mail in magazine and book offices, but some authors have already begun to send them by **modem** (modulator-de-modulator), a device that connects to a computer so that the machine can send and receive messages over telephone lines. Other authors use **fax** (fac-simile) machines that send copies of printed documents or illustrations. Gone are the days of laborious paste-ups of text and art. Illustrations and graphics designs can be generated by computer, and the designer can preview layouts on a computer screen in a matter of minutes.

Desktop publishing programs for even small computers have already led to professional looking short-run, special-interest magazines and self-published books. Even schools have gotten into the act. Many now use such programs to produce school newspapers or magazines and as an adjunct to reading and writing classes. Students can create their own magazines and books and, with the help of a copy machine, run off copies for proud friends and relatives.

Commercial publishers are already edging into publishing without print-ing—in other words, offering books and other information services on disk. Some offer "personalized" books that plug a child's name into a story told on the home computer. Others put encyclopedias on disk. Some educational publishers are investigating **active documents**—computerized textbooks that alter themselves to fit the abilities of the students using them.

Already many libraries and commercial **data bases**—information services—offer paperless magazines. At the computer terminal you tap in, say, "bicycle races," and the service scans an index and gives you the titles and sources of articles on this topic. You can call any you like to the screen. If the computer is attached to a printer, you can also receive copies of the articles you want to save.

Work is also being done on personalized newspapers. Perhaps in the near future, your newspaper will have all its stories—which will probably number more than can now be printed—available on computer. From your home or library computer, you can call for headlines or for any type of story. You could even program your computer to print out automatically the kinds of stories you know you're interested in—comic strips by three of your favorite artists, for instance, or movie reviews and advice columns, stories on football and tennis, or reports on the environment and education.

1. What computer information services do your school and community libraries use now? Do classes or clubs use word processing equipment?

2. Do the families of any class members subscribe to an on-line (computer-accessed) information service like Prodigy or GEnie? If so, have those students describe what services are available and how their families use them. Or pick up brochures from a local computer store for the class to examine.

# Audio/Video Technology

Over time, television sets and radios have become bigger and better—and smaller and better. Today consumers can choose from products that range from big-screen color stereo systems to tiny portables that fit in a pocket.

Some advances in audio/video technology have improved the quality of the broadcast; others have changed people's habits. Television watchers, for example, used to stick with one network for the evening because getting up to turn the channel was too much trouble. The introduction of the remote control changed those habits. Now people zap through twenty or thirty channels in a matter of minutes to find something they like. Or they "graze" all evening long, watching a few minutes of this, a few minutes of that. Or they use commercial time to cruise for other possibilities. Those with **state-of-the-art** (the most sophisticated available) equipment watch a split screen, say a sitcom on the major screen and a football game on the inset. If something good shapes up in the game, they can, with a flick of the control in their hand, bring it to the big screen.

As you have seen, one way movie companies increase their profits despite a decline in theater attendance is to make their movies available on video-cassette or compact disk. For a fraction of the cost of a theater movie, people can now watch movies with a VCR (videocassette recorder) or disc player attached to their television sets. And just around the corner is HDTV—high-definition television sets that produce images as clear as those in movies and sound as sharp as that on CDs. Recording companies are already working on music videos that fit the new format so that they'll be ready when home equipment is. Very soon you'll be able to visit famous nightclubs from your living room, watching hour-long videos of reggae, jazz, or pop.

Also just appearing are VCRs that automatically cut out commercials. Such a prospect makes advertisers nervous; they are already concerned about viewers who tape programs and then zip—fast forward—through the commercials. The networks are nervous, too: If viewers can block commercials, advertising prices will have to go down.

Another fertile area of recording technology is in **holography**—photography that uses laser light to create a three-dimensional image. So far holography is used only for special effects in places like Disney World or sales conventions, but who knows? Tomorrow's movies may be projected around you instead of in front of you.

Computer animation is already making inroads. Advertisers were the first to see the potential of **CGI**—computer-generated imagery. Many of the startling images you see in commercials are the result of this technology. It is also being used in the production of animated cartoons. The artist draws two pictures— the beginning and the end of a motion—and the computer fills in the steps between. And the computer "paints" the pictures, eliminating time-consuming hand inking.

Personal media are also being affected by the new technologies. While most families still record important moments with a still camera, a growing number are turning to **camcorders** (videotape cameras) to capture baby's first steps, sis's graduation, and junior's wedding. Others are experimenting in more creative ways, in effect crafting their own videos—and finding a national audience on television shows built around bloopers, humorous performances, and video magic.

With a computer connected to a music synthesizer, you can even create music that sounds like a full orchestra—or like nothing on earth. Saxophones, violins, guitars, as well as hisses, hums, flutters, and special effects like echoes, chorusing, and wave shifting—all can be produced at home, if you have the right equipment.

**A**ctivity **3**

1. If you have remote control television and a VCR, describe how you use them. Do you zap, graze, cruise, and mute? Why? One survey found that half of young adult viewers routinely watch two shows at once, zapping back and forth between them; 20 percent keep an eye on a third channel. Does that pattern describe you? Do you find you can keep track of more than one show, or do you just watch for interesting scenes?

2. If some class members use camcorders or synthesizers, have them demonstrate their use and show samples of their efforts.

## Multimedia and Interactive Media

In this book you have read about each of the media independently, but in the future you are apt to find yourself in a multimedia society.

Instead of in a family room or living room, family activity in the future is likely to gravitate around a media center. Here will be a computer, a printer, a big-screen television, superb audio equipment, and a telephone all interconnected. Part of the computer system might be a **CD-ROM** (compact disc—read-only memory) reader, and with this you will be able to pluck whole libraries, concert halls, and theaters from the disks on your shelves.

Or perhaps you don't want to bother owning all those disks. No matter—already through information services like Prodigy or GEnie, you can connect your home computer to databases, go shopping, buy stocks, pay bills, take lessons, or play games. Perhaps soon, you will be able to call up movies, television programs, concerts, or books from new kinds of central libraries.

Computer games and educational programs already allow for feedback from you—different things happen depending on what you do. Interactive TV now being tested will put you in the director's chair. Say you're watching a baseball game. You'll be able to choose from among four images of the action—

Getting Started in Mass Media

maybe a panoramic shot of the field, a slow-motion replay of a great catch, a shot of the scoreboard with stats and scores of other games, or a close-up of the batter. An exercise show asks you to choose your own workout; a comedy show offers you a choice of topics; an advice show answers your questions.

Interactive TV news is also being tested. With this system, a command from your remote control will bring you more detail on any of the stories you've just seen. Interactive video disks are also on the way. Say you rent a travelogue on France. With your remote control, you can ask for a TV tour of certain cities, stroll through public gardens, find out the admission price to a specific museum. With an electronic catalog, you could ask for a demonstration of a new toy, and on your television set watch a child playing with it.

And coming soon, you may be able to talk back to your television set. The cable television system in most areas is already capable of two-way communication, though put to little use so far. But perhaps in the near future, you'll be able to rate TV shows as soon as you watch them. And talk about participatory democracy—think how "turnout" would increase if voters could signal their choices for political office from their homes! Mechanisms against fraud would have to be developed, but the technology is ready when society is.

One form of interactive television, called **videotext,** could provide services similar to the on-line information services computer users are already using. With a TV, a decoder box, and a keypad, videotext users could call up information, handle their banking, make travel arrangements, or order their meals in advance from a local restaurant.

In business circles **teleconferencing** is already common. The service allows a number of people in different offices or even different cities to talk together on the phone. The next step is **videoconferencing,** in which participants can see each other on TV screens. Already used in some schools and colleges, videoconferencing enables students to take courses with a teacher at another school. And your home media center may have the same capability—the family reunion of the future may involve everyone staying in their own homes but linking together through their televisions!

Because of the information transfer media that already exist—computer networks, modems, and fax machines—a growing number of people can work for a company without leaving home. An accountant, for example, can receive the day's activity reports by modem, manipulate the data as required, and enter the final figures in the main office computer.

Many people already use this equipment, too, just to chat—computer bulletin boards allow writers, jazz buffs, sports fans, or members of any interest group to "talk" to each other anywhere in the country. Travel club members exchange tips and ideas. Professionals in many fields use their computers to "discuss" the latest developments in their field. Some companies already use **e-mail**—electronic mail. Perhaps in the future your address will be a computer number like a telephone number; you'll receive your letters and bills in an electronic mailbox.

This media center could also become the brains of the house. Architects are talking about the "smart house" whose central computer could operate a security system, monitor utility use, turn off lights automatically, provide menu selections and cook food, track your finances, and much more.

All of this may sound like science fiction, but in fact most of the technology that could turn these ideas into reality already exists. You'll be a witness as more and more of them become commonplace. Already some colleges require incoming students to have their own computers; others have terminals in every dorm room. Laptop computers are already widespread. Tomorrow's students may not need backpacks for textbooks and notebooks; instead, they'll carry their own laptops with a little case full of disks.

Someday you'll tell your children stories of the days when you had television in one room, the telephone in another, the stereo off in the corner, and there was no computer at all. Your children will roll their eyes in disbelief. "How did you *live?*" they'll demand as they go off to do their homework: a report on the pyramids that will include a video tour of the monuments; full-color architectural drawings showing how they were built; and their own commentary spoken against a background of ancient music. They'll prepare this report in their own bedrooms, using their computer to tap into vast libraries of audio, video, and print resources. If you show them the report you did when you were in school—the three handwritten pages with pictures you cut out of magazines—they'll be amazed how easy it was "in the old days" to get an A.

**Activity 4**

1. Video telephones are just around the corner. Would owning one affect your telephone habits? Would you want a button that lets you blank out the video?

2. Do you use computers now? At school? At home? Do you play computer games? How else do you use computers?

3. How might the new interactive media affect school—students, teachers, tests, and lessons? Consider two possibilities: (1) Students continue to come to a central school, but individual work stations, classrooms, and libraries will be wired into computers and audio/video equipment. (2) Students go to "school" via their home media center. A computer tutor keeps track of their progress in reading and math; at least once a day, they teleconference with other students to discuss a novel or a history lesson; they do a simulated dissection of a frog on their television screen, with the computer guiding their "cuts," explaining what they see, and pointing out their errors.

4. Brainstorm about how the changes described above might affect the content of the media. Will there still be network TV shows in the future? Will radio still concentrate on music and talk? Will printed books exist at all? Will advertising exist? If not, how will businesses provide information about their goods and services? What other changes do you foresee?

# Talking It Over

When personal computers first appeared, some forecasters predicted that almost every home would have one by 1990. That prediction did not come true. While the technology for the ideas described above is either here or coming, no one knows how many people will buy into it. Consider what you know about media and about people. Then decide which of the following statements better reflects your judgment. Discuss your opinions with your classmates.

■ I believe change is coming, and fast. People like gadgets, and they like convenience. Therefore, it's very important for young people to understand mass media and computers. If anything, high technology will play an even bigger role in their lives tomorrow.

■ Sure, computers are important in business and other fields. But I don't think the majority of people will buy into these multimedia homes. Most people will continue to use media as they do now and pay no attention to computers and interactive media.

# And the Bad News Is . . .

Although many benefits will result from the coming world of multimedia, there are some dangers as well.

That family media center? Yes, it puts the world's information and entertainment resources right into the home—but might we become a nation of hermits? Would people's social urges still take them out to meetings, parties, restaurants, theaters? Or would the convenience of having most of these services at home outweigh those urges?

That two-way television? The cable company can already monitor what you watch, if it wanted to. How will we protect people's privacy when computer links become even more widespread? Do we really want computers collecting information on what we watch, what we read, what we buy—and how we vote?

It's already happening. George Orwell's novel *1984* raised the specter of Big Brother, a giant government that watched people even in their homes. Today, cameras watch you as you bank, as you shop—perhaps as you go to school. Today, your name ends up on mailing lists generated by computers that track where you live, what magazines you subscribe to, what catalogs you order from, how you use your credit cards. In the future, computers may track you from birth to death—your school records, work history, health records, finances, driving record, interests.

In the future we may begin to worry not about one Big Brother, but many of them—government agencies, media giants, advertisers—who know more about us than we want them to.

**Activity 5**

1. Make a list of the possible benefits of the new multimedia world. Consider individual knowledge and entertainment, but also consider the impact on business, science, medicine, the arts, the environment.
2. Suggest ways for society to avoid the dangers described above.

## Summary

The history of media is in part the history of the technology that makes it possible. The twentieth century has witnessed explosive change in media, and the twenty-first century will witness even greater change. Audio, video, and print equipment has improved dramatically, and the computer has further expanded the range and capabilities of that equipment. Links between this equipment and the telephone already exist, and the future will see further expansion of multimedia and interactive functions. Homes, schools, and businesses may be transformed by the ability to tap into vast information sources and to transmit information wherever there are telephone and cable wires to carry it. These changes offer opportunities, but they also pose the danger of declining social contact and loss of privacy.

## VIEWPOINT

**Issac Asimov** was born in Russia but grew up in America, where he earned a doctorate in chemistry. He is one of the most prolific of American writers, having written over 250 books, most notably science fiction and science. He has won every major award in science fiction; both his robot stories and his *Foundation* series are considered classics in the field. In "The Fun They Had," he shows how some of the new technologies could affect education.

# The Fun They Had

### Isaac Asimov

Margie even wrote about it that night in her diary. On the page headed 17 May, 2155, she wrote, "Today Tommy found a real book!"

It was a very old book. Margie's grandfather once said that when he was a little boy *his* grandfather told him that there was a time when all stories were printed on paper.

They turned the pages, which were yellow and crinkly, and it was awfully funny to read words that stood still instead of moving the way they were supposed to—on a screen, you know. And then, when they turned back to the page before, it had the same words on it that it had had when they read it the first time.

"Gee," said Tommy, "what a waste. When you're through with the book, you just throw it away, I guess. Our television screen must have had a million books on it and it's good for plenty more. I wouldn't throw *it* away."

"Same with mine," said Margie. She was eleven and hadn't seen as many telebooks as Tommy had. He was thirteen.

She said, "Where did you find it?"

"In my house." He pointed without looking, because he was busy reading. "In the attic."

"What's it about?"

"School."

Margie was scornful. "School? What's there to write about school? I hate school." Margie always hated school, but now she hated it more than ever. The mechanical teacher had been giving her test after test in geography and she had been doing worse and worse until her mother had shaken her head sorrowfully and sent for the County Inspector.

He was a round little man with a red face and a whole box of tools with dials and wires. He smiled at her and gave her an apple, then took the teacher apart. Margie had hoped he wouldn't know how to put it together again, but he knew how all right and after an hour or so, there it was again, large and black and ugly with a big screen on which all the lessons were shown and the questions were asked. That wasn't so bad. The part she hated most was the slot where she had to put homework and test papers. She always had to write them out in a punch code they made her learn when she was six years old, and the mechanical teacher calculated the mark in no time.

The Inspector had smiled after he was finished and patted her head. He said to her mother, "It's not the little girl's fault, Mrs. Jones. I think the geography sector was geared a little too quick. Those things happen sometimes. I've slowed it up to an average ten-year level.

Actually, the overall pattern of her progress is quite satisfactory." And he patted Margie's head again.

Margie was disappointed. She had been hoping they would take the teacher away altogether. They had once taken Tommy's teacher away for nearly a month because the history sector had blanked out completely.

So she said to Tommy, "Why would anyone write about school?"

Tommy looked at her with very superior eyes. "Because it's not our kind of school, stupid. This is the old kind of school that they had hundreds and hundreds of years ago." He added loftily, pronouncing the word carefully, "*Centuries* ago."

Margie was hurt. "Well, I don't know what kind of school they had all that time ago." She read the book over his shoulder for a while, then said, "Anyway, they had a teacher."

"Sure they had a teacher, but it wasn't a *regular* teacher. It was a man."

"A man? How could a man be a teacher?"

"Well, he just told the boys and girls things and gave them homework and asked them questions."

"A man isn't smart enough."

"Sure he is. My father knows as much as my teacher."

"He can't. A man can't know as much as a teacher."

"He knows almost as much I betcha."

Margie wasn't prepared to dispute that. She said, "I wouldn't want a strange man in my house to teach me."

Tommy screamed with laughter, "You don't know much, Margie. The teachers didn't live in the house. They had a special building and all the kids went there."

"And all the kids learned the same thing?"

"Sure, if they were the same age."

"But my mother says a teacher has to be adjusted to fit the mind of each boy and girl it teaches and that each kid has to be taught differently."

"Just the same they didn't do it that way then. If you don't like it, you don't have to read the book."

"I didn't say I didn't like it," Margie said quickly. She wanted to read about those funny schools.

They weren't even half finished when Margie's mother called, "Margie! School!"

Margie looked up. "Not yet, Mama."

"Now," said Mrs. Jones. "And it's probably time for Tommy, too."

Margie said to Tommy, "Can I read the book some more with you after school?"

"Maybe," he said, nonchalantly. He walked away whistling, the dusty old book tucked beneath his arm.

Margie went into the schoolroom. It was right next to her bedroom, and the mechanical teacher was on and waiting for her. It was always on at the same time every day except Saturday and Sunday, because her mother said little girls learned better if they learned at regular hours.

The screen was lit up, and it said: "Today's arithmetic lesson is on the addition of proper fractions. Please insert yesterday's homework in the proper slot."

Margie did so with a sigh. She was thinking about the old schools they had when her grandfather's grandfather was a little boy. All the kids from the whole neighborhood came, laughing and shouting in the schoolyard, sitting together in the schoolroom, going home together at the end of the day. They learned the same things so they could help one another on the homework and talk about it.

And the teachers were people . . .

The mechanical teacher was flashing on the screen: "When we add the fractions 1/2 and 1/4—"

Margie was thinking about how the kids must have loved it in the old days. She was thinking about the fun they had. ∎

## ☞ Your Turn

1. Asimov shows one way interactive media might change education. Write a short story about another way.

2. Write a humorous essay about school today, showing how it could be improved with multimedia and interactive media.

# Glossary

**A&R (artists and repertory) executive:** A producer working for a record company who oversees the selection of performers and music.

**Academy awards:** Annual awards given for achievements in the film industry—Best Picture, Best Director, and so on. The Oscar is a gold-plated statue presented to the winners.

**ACE awards:** Annual awards for excellence in original cable programs presented by National Cable Television Association.

**Active documents:** Computerized textbooks that alter themselves to fit the abilities of the students using them.

**Advance:** Money paid on anticipated royalties to a writer or recording artist upon signing a contract or completing a work.

**Advertorial:** An advertisement in a newspaper or magazine that looks like a news story or an article.

**Advocacy group:** A group that lobbies government and the media in support of or in opposition to a particular point of view.

**Affiliate:** A local radio or television station operating under a contractual arrangement with a network.

**Bandwagon:** A propaganda technique urging people take an action because everyone else is.

**Beat reporter:** A reporter assigned to a particular news source (like a police station or city hall) or field (like science or economics).

**Blurb:** Information on a book cover designed to make the book sound appealing.

**Bureau:** A branch office of a newspaper or wire service in an important news area.

**Byline:** A reporter's name on a story or article.

**Camcorder:** A hand-held video camera.

**CD-ROM:** Compact disc, read-only memory; a computer disk that stores great amounts of information.

**CGI:** Computer-generated imagery; a computer program that facilitates cartooning and other graphic work.

**Chronological story:** A news story relating events in the order they occurred.

**Cinematography:** Camera work, including choice of shots, focus, filters, angle, and movement.

**Classified ads:** Newspaper and magazine ads sold by the line and sorted into various categories.

**Clio awards:** Annual awards given to outstanding television and radio commercials.

**Columnist:** A newspaper or magazine writer who expresses his or her opinions about different subjects.

**Commentary:** An expression of opinion.

**Compatible programming:** Scheduling similar programs in a time segment in order to hold a group of viewers.

**Composite story:** A news story that links several related events.

**Correspondent:** A news reporter stationed away from the home office.

**Counterprogramming:** Offering something different from another network in order to draw off viewers.

**Data base:** A computer service that allows access to various kinds of information.

**Death notice:** A paid announcement in a newspaper about someone's death.

**Demo:** A demonstration record or tape.

**Demographics:** The study of group characteristics, including such factors as age, gender, income, and education.

**Display ads:** Advertisements sold by size and location in a newspaper or magazine; distinguished from classified ads.

**Docudrama:** A dramatic presentation based on a true story.

**Documentary:** A factual program on radio or television, often dealing with current controversy.

**Editorial:** Commentary that represents the official opinion of the management of a newspaper, magazine, or broadcasting station.

**Editorialize:** To inject opinion inappropriately into a news story.

**Emmy:** An annual award given to achievement in television, such as Best Comedy Series and Best Documentary.

**E-mail:** Electronic mail, sent via one computer to another.

**Fax:** Facsimile machine, which sends an exact copy of a document to another machine via telephone lines.

**FCC:** Federal Communications Commission, the government agency that regulates the radio and television.

**Feature story:** In a newspaper, a story that provides background or entertainment rather than hard news; in a magazine, the most important article.

**Feedback:** A response to a communication.

**Five W's and H:** *Who, what, where, when, why,* and *how;* key questions whose answers are incorporated in a news story.

**Format:** The overall appearance and makeup of printed material; the type of programming emphasized by a radio station.

**Free-lancer:** A writer, artist, or photographer who sells his or her work to various media.

**Gatekeeper:** An editor who decides which news stories will be printed or broadcast.

**General assignment reporter:** A reporter who may be assigned to cover any news event.

**Genre:** In publishing, a particular type of book or magazine, such as science-fiction or mystery.

**Glittering generality:** A propaganda technique associating positive but vague words or images with a product or idea.

**Grammy:** Annual awards by the recording industry to outstanding performers.

**HDTV:** High-definition television; a system which produces high-quality television images.

**Heartstrings:** A propaganda technique based on appeals to the emotions.

**Holography:** Three-dimensional photography.

**Informational ad:** One which presents actual information about the product or service.

**Infomercial:** Paid programming; a block of television time purchased by an advertiser to promote a product or service.

**Institutional ad:** One designed to foster good will about an organization or an industry.

**Interactive TV:** A television capable of two-way interaction.

**Interference:** Competing messages that disrupt communication.

**Interpretive report:** A news story that provides explanations or analysis in addition to hard facts.

**Inverted pyramid style:** A writing style that presents the most important information first; the next most important information, second; and the least important, last.

**Investigative report:** A news story exposing corruption or incompetence in government, military, or industry.

**Journal:** A magazine targeted to the members of a profession.

**Lead:** The first paragraph of a news story, which conveys the most important information.

**Literary agent:** One who for a fee negotiates with publishers on behalf of an author.

**Madison Avenue:** Street in New York City associated with the advertising industry.

**Mass media:** Those means of communication which reach a very large audience.

**Media:** The plural of *medium;* agencies of mass communication in general.

**Modem:** A device that sends information from one computer to another via telephone wires.

**Name calling:** A propaganda technique which involves saying negative things about the competition.

**Narrowcasting:** Programming targeted to a smaller audience than a regular broadcast.

**Novelization:** The creation of a novel based on a movie or television script.

**Obituary:** A news story about the death of a person.

**Option:** The purchase of the right to film a book at some future date.

**Op-ed page:** The page opposite the editorial page in a newspaper, typically a forum for other opinion pieces.

**Overload:** A communication problem resulting from too many messages received at one time.

**Pilot:** A sample for a proposed television program or recording.

**Plain folks:** A propaganda technique that stresses the appeal of the product or idea to ordinary people.

**Press association:** Same as wire service.

**Press release:** A story submitted to the media by a group, agency, or business, seeking favorable publicity.

**Product differentiation ad:** An advertisement showing how a product or service differs favorably from the competition.

**Propaganda:** Methods of persuasion based on emotional rather than rational reasons.

**Public service ad:** One designed to further a social good.

**Pulitzer Prizes:** Annual cash awards given to outstanding achievements in journalism, literature, drama, and music.

**Rating:** The percentage of the viewing population that watched a particular television show or tuned in to a particular radio station.

**Review:** Commentary which evaluates the worth of an artistic production.

**Royalty:** The percentage of the price of a book or record that goes to the author or artist.

**Screenplay:** The script of a movie or television program.

**Self-publishing:** Production and distribution of a book other than through a publishing company.

**Sensationalism:** An overemphasis on crime, violence, gossip, scandal, and shock-value stories.

**Sidebar:** A short, separate item accompanying a news story or magazine article and presenting additional information.

**Slant:** A news story giving a one-sided impression of an event.

**Slush pile:** Unsolicited manuscripts (ones which were not commissioned) sent to a publisher or producer.

**Standards and practices:** A committee within a television network that reviews the fairness and principles of the network's offerings.

**State of the art:** Equipment that is the most up-to-date available.

**Straight news:** A factual account free of the writer's opinion, interpretation, or analysis.

**Stringer:** A part-time correspondent for a news medium.

**Subsidy publishing:** Arrangement by which a writer pays a publishing company (subsidizes it) to print his or her book; also known as the vanity press.

**Syndicate:** A company which sells the work of free-lance writers and artists to newspapers or magazines, radio shows for broadcast, or television series for rerun.

**Synthesizer:** A computer-controlled device that produces sound and music.

**Tabloid:** A newspaper about half the size of a regular newspaper; a newspaper which deals in sensationalism.

**Teleconference:** A meeting between a number of people in different places linked by telephone lines.

**Testimonial:** A propaganda technique in which a well-known person or an expert recommends a product or an idea.

**Trade book:** One intended for the general public, as distinguished from a textbook.

**Trade magazine:** One intended for practitioners in a trade, like plumbers, electricians, or restaurateurs.

**Vanity press:** Same as subsidy publishing.

**VCR:** Video cassette recorder; a machine that records and plays videotapes.

**Videoconference:** A meeting of people in different locations linked by telephone lines that allows participants to see each other on television screens.

**Videotext:** An interactive electronic system that transmits information on telephone lines or cable to a subscriber's television.

**Watchdog:** The function of the press to watch for and report on misdeeds by government, the military, or business.

**Whistle blower:** An employee within an organization who reveals the misdeeds of others to his or her superiors, government agencies, or the media.

**Wire service:** A news-gathering organization which sells its work to the media.

# Index